THE
CHOW CHOW

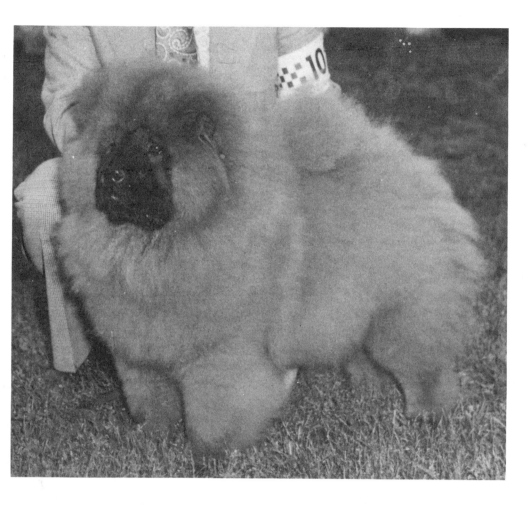

BY ANNA KATHERINE NICHOLAS

**Featuring special sections by
Desmond J. Murphy**

Front cover: Ch. Don Lee Chowtime, owned by Desmond J. Murphy and Susie Donelly. Photo courtesy of Dr. Samuel Draper.

Title page photo: Ch. Car Mar Pucker for Dusten as a puppy in 1974 making a Best Sr. Puppy in Non-Sporting Group win. Handled by John Cox for himself and Dusten Cox, Dusten's Chow Chows, Sharon, Connecticut.

Distributed in the UNITED STATES by T.F.H. Publications, Inc., 211 West Sylvania Avenue, Neptune City, NJ 07753; in CANADA by H & L Pet Supplies Inc., 27 Kingston Crescent, Kitchener, Ontario N2B 2T6; Rolf C. Hagen Ltd., 3225 Sartelon Street, Montreal 382 Quebec; in ENGLAND by T.F.H. Publications Limited, 4 Kier Park, Ascot, Berkshire SL5 7DS; in AUSTRALIA AND THE SOUTH PACIFIC by T.F.H. (Australia) Pty. Ltd., Box 149, Brookvale 2100 N.S.W., Australia; in NEW ZEALAND by Ross Haines & Son, Ltd., 18 Monmouth Street, Grey Lynn, Auckland 2 New Zealand; in SINGAPORE AND MALAYSIA by MPH Distributors (S) Pte., Ltd., 601 Sims Drive, # 03/07/21, Singapore 1438; in the PHILIPPINES by Bio-Research, 5 Lippay Street, San Lorenzo Village, Makati Rizal; in SOUTH AFRICA by Multipet Pty. Ltd., 30 Turners Avenue, Durban 4001. Published by T.F.H. Publications Inc., Ltd. the British Crown Colony of Hong Kong.

Dedication
To all who admire and love the Chow Chow

Contents

About the Author 7

Chapter 1: ORIGIN OF THE CHOW CHOW 11

Chapter 2: THE CHOW CHOW IN GREAT BRITAIN 15

Chapter 3: EARLY HISTORY IN THE UNITED STATES 25
First Champion. . .Early Kennels. . .The Chow Chow Club

Chapter 4: KENNELS IN THE UNITED STATES 51
AHSO Fan-C. . .Al De Bear. . .Cabaret. . .Cedar Creek. . .
Dusten's. . .Kamara. . .Kim-Sha. . .Ky-Lin. . .Liontamer
. . .Palm. . .Sa-Mi. . .Sho-Tay. . .Shanghai. . .Sunswept. . .
Taichung. . .Wu Li

Chapter 5: CHOW CHOWS IN CANADA 97
British Columbia. . .Ontario. . .Quebec

Chapter 6: CHOW CHOWS IN AUSTRALIA 109

Chapter 7: STANDARDS OF THE BREED 115
American Standard. . .British and Australian Standard. . .
Interpretation of the American Chow Chow Standard

Chapter 8: THE SMOOTH-COATED CHOW CHOW 127

Chapter 9: THE PURCHASE OF YOUR DOG OR PUPPY. . . .131

Chapter 10: THE CARE OF YOUR PUPPY. 155
Preparing for Your Puppy's Arrival. . .Joining the Family
. . .Socializing and Training Your New Puppy. . .Feeding
Your Dog

Chapter 11: CORRECT GROOMING AND BATHING OF YOUR
CHOW CHOW. 197
Grooming the Adult. . .Grooming the Puppy. . .Bathing

Chapter 12: THE MAKING OF A SHOW DOG 205
    General Considerations. . .Match Shows. . .Point Shows
    . . .Junior Showmanship Competition. . .Pre-Show Prepa-
    ration for Your Dog and You. . .Enjoying the Dog Show

Chapter 13: YOUR DOG AND OBEDIENCE 243

Chapter 14: BREEDING YOUR CHOW CHOW. 247
    The Brood Bitch. . .The Stud Dog. . .Pregnancy, Whelp-
    ing, and the Litter

Chapter 15: TRAVELING WITH YOUR DOG. 273

Chapter 16: RESPONSIBILITIES OF BREEDERS AND
    OWNERS 277

Index 282

About the Author

Since early childhood, Anna Katherine Nicholas has been involved with dogs. Her first pets were a Boston Terrier, an Airedale, and a German Shepherd. Then, in 1925, came the first of the Pekingese—a gift from a friend who raised them. Now her home is shared with a Miniature Poodle and a dozen or so Beagles, including her noted Best in Show dog and National Specialty winner, Champion Rockaplenty's Wild Oats, a Gold Certificate sire (one of the breed's truly great stud dogs), who as a show dog was Top Beagle in the Nation in 1973. She also owns Champion Foyscroft True Blue Lou, Foyscroft Aces Are Wild, and in co-ownership with Marcia Foy, who lives with her, Champion Foyscroft Triple Mitey Migit.

Miss Nicholas is best known throughout the Dog Fancy as a writer and as a judge. Her first magazine article, published in *Dog News* magazine around 1930, was about Pekingese; and this was followed by a widely acclaimed breed column, "Peeking at the Pekingese" which appeared for at least two decades, originally in *Dogdom*, then, following the demise of that publication, in *Popular Dogs*. During the 1940's she was Boxer columnist for *Pure-Bred Dogs/American Kennel Gazette* and for *Boxer Briefs*. More recently many of her articles, geared to interest fanciers of every breed, have appeared in *Popular Dogs, Pure-Bred Dogs/American Kennel Gazette, Show Dogs, Dog Fancy*, and *The World of the Working Dog*. Currently she is a featured regular columnist in *Kennel Review, Dog World, Canine Chronicle* and *The Dog Fancier* (Canadian). Her *Dog World* column, "Here, There and Everywhere," was the Dog Writers Association of America winner of the Best Series in a Dog Magazine Award for 1979.

It was during the late 1930's that Miss Nicholas' first book, *The Pekingese*, appeared, published by and written at the request of the Judy Publishing Company. This book completely sold out and is now a collector's item, as is her *The Skye Terrier Book*, which was published by the Skye Terrier Club of America during the early 1960's.

In 1970 Miss Nicholas won the Dog Writers Association of America award for the Best Technical Book of the Year with her *Nicholas Guide to Dog Judging*. Then in 1979 the revision of this book again won the Dog Writers Association of America Best Technical Book Award, the first time ever that a revision has been so honored by this association.

In the early 1970's, Miss Nicholas co-authored, with Joan Brearley, five breed books which were published by T.F.H. Publications, Inc. These were *This is the Bichon Frise, The Wonderful World of Beagles and Beagling* (winner of a Dog Writers Association of America Honorable Mention Award), *The Book of the Pekingese, The Book of the Boxer,* and *This is the Skye Terrier*.

During recent years, Miss Nicholas has been writing books consistently for T.F.H. These include *Successful Dog Show Exhibiting, The Book of the Rottweiler, The Book of the Poodle, The Book of the Labrador Retriever, The Book of the English Springer Spaniel, The Book of the Golden Retriever,* and *The Book of the German Shepherd Dog*. Most recently she has written *The Book of the Shetland Sheepdog,* another breed spectacular, and in the same series with the one you are now reading, *The Maltese, The Keeshond, The Cocker Spaniel,* and several additional titles. In the T.F.H. "KW" series, she has done *Rottweilers, Weimaraners,* and *Norwegian Elkhounds*. She has also supplied the American chapters for two English publications, imported by T.F.H., *The Staffordshire Bull Terrier* and *The Jack Russell Terrier*.

Miss Nicholas, in addition to her four Dog Writers Association of America awards, has on two occasions been honored with the *Kennel Review* "Winkie" as Dog Writer of the Year; and in both 1977 and 1982 she was recipient of the Gaines "Fido" award as Journalist of the Year in Dogs.

Her judging career began in 1934 at the First Company Governors' Foot Guard in Hartford, Connecticut, drawing the largest Pekingese entry ever assembled to date at this event. Presently she is approved to judge all Hounds, Terriers, Toys, and Non-Sporting Dogs; all Pointers, English and Gordon Setters, Vizslas, Weimaraners, and Wire-haired Pointing Griffons in Sporting breeds and, in Working Group, Boxers and Doberman Pinschers. In 1970 she became the third woman in history to judge Best in Show at the prestigious Westminster Kennel Club Dog Show, where she has officiated on some sixteen other occasions through the years. In addition to her numerous Westminster assignments, Miss Nicholas has judged at such other outstandingly important events as Santa Barbara, Trenton, Chicago In-

Ch. Don Lee Chowtime with his co-owner Desmond Murphy winning the Non-Sporting Group at Newton Kennel Club in 1978. Anna K. Nicholas, judge.

ternational, the Sportsmans in Canada, the Metropolitan in Canada, and Specialty Shows in several dozen breeds both in the United States and in Canada. She has judged in almost every one of the mainland United States and in four Canadian provinces, and her services are constantly sought in other countries.

Through the years, Miss Nicholas has held important offices in a great many all-breed and Specialty clubs. She still remains an honorary member of several of them.

Showing all the character of his breed, future champion Dre Don Sun King of Craglinden by Ch. Loy-Jean's Chi Yan Kid ex Ch. Loy-Jean's Sassi Lassi at one year of age in May 1968. Owned by Dr. Samuel Draper and Robert A. Hetherington, Jr.

Chapter 1

Origin of the Chow Chow

The Chow Chow is without a doubt one of our most ancient breeds of dog, with a background descended from progenitors who existed and were recognizable as such all the way back into the eleventh century B.C. These early dogs were of lion-like appearance, large and powerful, and distinguished by black tongues which are very rare among dog breeds throughout the world. These are the dogs who accompanied the Tartars on their invasion of China and who are known as the "man kou" or as the "Tartar Dogs."

It is believed that the Chow Chow's ancestors came originally from the Arctic Circle, from where they migrated to Siberia, Mongolia, and China. One school of thought is that these early dogs resulted from a crossing of the early Samoyed with the Mastiff from Tibet; on the other hand there are those who believe that the Chow was himself one of the "basic breeds," the ancestor rather than the descendant of the "northern type" dogs, which include the Samoyed, along with the Norwegian Elkhound, the Keeshond and the Pomeranian. Who is to say, beyond the fact that these breeds share with him a basic similarity of type, in what sequence their development so long ago took place?

The Chinese ancestors of the Chow Chow were basically hunting dogs and the only ones native to China. In the days of the great imperial hunts, they were used as both pointers and retrievers; and we have heard it stated that one Chinese emperor, with ten thousand huntsmen in his forces, kept at a time more than two thousand of these dogs to accompany his forces. Selective breeding of these dogs seemed unimportant to the majority, following the ending of these great hunts; and it was only thanks to a small number of the wealthy and the nobility that secret breeding of them continued, which probably saved the breed from extinction.

This lovely bitch, shown in the late 1960's, is Ky Lin's Quicksilver, by Ch. Ky Lin's Quintus ex Ky Lin's Cotton Candy. Owned by Audrey and Richard Meaney.

It is said that early Chow Chows, in addition to their hunting abilities, were used as herding dogs, keeping the flocks in their charge well under control, and as sled dogs. In other words, the original Chow Chows were useful working and hunting canines of strength and power.

Chow Chows have been depicted in various ways, on sculptures and on pottery since the Han Dynasty, about 150 B.C. Unfortunately, the Chinese emperors habitually and ruthlessly destroyed art and literature from the periods preceding their own. Were it not for this fact, who knows how much more evidence might have been found of the Chow Chow's antiquity?

The name "Chow Chow" has a variety of explanations. We think the most logical of them is that on his early voyages, when the first of the breed came by clipper ship from China to England, the dogs traveled in the hold of the ship where miscellaneous objects usually were stored. These objects were known as "Chow Chow" and the hold was known as "the Chow Chow hold." Since the dogs became part of the "Chow Chow" carried on these trips, does not it seem logical that the breed name might have originated there? It is also said that it has been taken from the Chinese word "Chaou," meaning "a dog of great strength," which of course might be the case.

Yum Yum of Broadhurst was a highly successful winning puppy in 1949. This beautiful owner-bred blue puppy was a daughter of Ch. Jo Jo Hanson ex Ho Han Keko of Broadhurst. Owned by Florence and Douglas Broadhurst of Redwood City, California.

Eng. Ch. Baytor Sasha with young Jennifer Westlake. This famous Chow, owned by Anita Westlake, Baytor Kennels, Teignmouth, Devon, England, is the sire of Eng. Ch. Baytor Flossie Flump who won the highest number of Challenge Certificates awarded any Chow in England during 1981; is himself an impressive winner in addition to being a renowned stud dog.

Chapter 2

The Chow Chow in Great Britain

It was as far back as 1780 that the first Chow Chows are said to have appeared in England. They were easily recognizable as such due to their unique blue-black tongue. From descriptions we have read, they also possessed the scowling expression, another Chow Chow characteristic which has retained its important role in correct breed type even until the present day.

Not until the 1860's, however, did the Chow's popularity and recognition in England really start to get under way. Handsome and impressive, these dogs were quick to arouse the admiration and the interest of nobility the moment they were introduced in social circles, with serious breeding of them commencing in several quarters.

The introduction of Chow Chows to England must be credited to the Earl of Lonsdale who became one of England's leading supporters of the breed, an interest he retained throughout his lifetime. This gentleman, noted for his great love of all animals, was given a Chow Chow on one of his frequent trips to the Far East, which he in turn, upon reaching home, presented to relatives, the Marquis and Marchioness of Huntley. So charmed did all of them become with this dog that Lord Hugh (the Earl of Lonsdale) was commissioned to bring more of them back to England, which he did on subsequent trips.

The Marchioness of Huntley became England's first notable breeder of Chow Chows, and her dogs were a very important influence on future generations. Among her importations was a dog known as Periodot (spelling variable with "Peridot") by whom she bred a son, Peridot II, sold to Lady Faudel Phillips. Peridot II goes down in history as having been the winner of the first truly important award gained by an English Chow Chow, that of Best in Show at the big and prestigious Ladies Kennel Club Championship Show on June 8th 1895.

Portuguese Ch. Baytor Sunset Sue, litter sister to British Ch. Baytor Scarlet Jade, by Baytor Midnight ex Baytor Sweet Gypsy Rose, an important international winner with numerous honors included in an exciting record. Owned by Mr. Fernando Rodriques and bred by Mrs. A.H. Westlake, Teignmouth, Devon, England.

Lady Faudel Phillips was the daughter of another of the pioneer British Chow Chow breeders, Lady Granville Gordon. As the former Armyne Gordon, she grew up sharing her parents' keen interest in and involvement with Chows, eventually inheriting all of their dogs. Her kennel was known as "Amwell"—a kennel identification synonymous with correct type and quality in Great Britain's early Chow Chow world, continuing until the time of her death in 1943. The well-known Chow Chow authority, Percy Whitaker, was kennel manager here from 1919 until the kennel was closed. Many notable Chows came from Amwell.

It was the Granville Gordons who produced the first British-bred Chow Chow to gain the championship title. This was a dog named Champion Blue Blood, of red parentage but himself a blue. Combined with their daughter having been the owner of Peridot II, just on these two dogs alone one can see the quality of Chow campaigned by these two generations of fanciers and realize their importance in the early British history of the breed.

Queen Victoria is said to have added a Chow Chow, imported from China, to her very large and diversified canine family in about 1865, a sure indication that the breed would flourish among British aristocracy.

It was in 1880 that the first Chow Chow was exhibited at the Crystal Palace Dog Show in London. This was a black bitch, Chinese Puzzle, owned by W.K. Taunton. In 1893, Chow Chows for the first time received their own classification at a British dog show, on December 10th and 11th at the London Aquarium. Previously they had been eligible only for the "foreign dog" class.

The first Chow Chow was registered in the Stud Book by the Kennel Club in England in 1894.

Ch. Baytor Apricot Silk, noted English winning Chow by Baytor Rajah Kuan ex Baytor Haunted Moon. Breeder-owner-handler Mrs. Anita Westlake, Teignmouth, Devon, England.

July 1st 1895 was the important date upon which a gathering of Chow Chow fanciers assembled in London for the purpose of discussing the organization of what was to become the Chow Chow Club. In attendance were, of course, Lady Granville Gordon and her daughter Lady Faudel Phillips, along with Mr. W. Temple, serving as chairman; Miss Ella Casella, a very highly respected and knowledgeable authority on the breed; Mrs. Burgess, Mr. and Mrs. Janvrin Dickson, Mrs. Fitswilliam, Mrs. Arthur James, and Mrs. Onken. At that time a "scale of points" (standard for the breed) was drawn up which has remained effective, with only very minor changes, until the present. The current British standard can be found in a later chapter.

Following the aforementioned meeting, the Chow Chow Club received its official recognition from the Kennel Club and subsequently staged its first Specialty Show at Westminster, London. Challenge Certificates for the breed were granted the following year, in 1896, the first of which were won by Lady Granville Gordon with her dog, Blue Blood, and by W.H.R. Temple with his bitch, Blue Bell.

Probably the biggest winner of this period was an imported dog, Champion Chow VIII, who was the first of the breed to gain a championship title in Great Britain. So excellent was this dog's conformation that he is said to have been the Chow Chow from whom the standard of the breed was written; but it is also said that he had somewhat of a personality problem evidenced by a tendency to bite. The dog changed ownership a number of times—perhaps the reason for his poor disposition, or perhaps it was vice versa! Anyway, he was handled by Jack Holgate through several different ownerships and lived at Mr. Holgate's kennel.

As already mentioned, Champion Blue Blood was the first *English-bred* Chow Chow to become a champion. A blue bitch, Champion Leyswood Blue Bell, was the first bitch; and Champion T'ien, owned by Miss Ella Casella, was the first red champion bitch.

Other noteworthy Chows and Chow people around the turn of the century included Mrs. Scaramanga. She brought back to England, after a long visit to India in 1898, a black Chow Chow dog, Hak Kwhy. He was destined to become an immediate success in the show ring; he won a total of fourteen Challenge Certificates by the time of retirement. This was the beginning of the famed Kwhy kennel, which later included such dogs as Champion Foo Kwhy, Champion Wiggles (winner of eighteen Challenge Certificates) and Champion Red Craze (sired by Champion Shylock who came to the United States).

Amwell Kennels had several noted winners immediately prior to World War I, as did Hildewell Kennels, belonging to Mrs. F.B. Moore. Miss Anna Peck had a worthy champion in Duchess of Nona.

At the close of the war, in 1919, when activity resumed in Britain's dog show world, two Chows immediately became dominant. They were a black dog owned by Lady Faudel Phillips, Champion Pusa of Amwell, and a red bitch owned by Mr. Allright, Champion Pickles, a daughter of the also well-known Champion Sinbad, both born in 1913. In 1919 Pickles was bred to Pusa, producing a litter which included

Winners of the Chow Chow Brace Class, handled by Miss Jennifer Westlake, age 14, were these litter sisters Baytor Blue Cobweb *(left)* and Champion Baytor Blue Star. Sire, Minhow Monty Blue of Baytor. Dam, Baytor Lucille. Breeder-owner, Mrs. Anita Westlake. Photo by Denis A. Lewis.

Ch. Baytor Blue Star, by Minhow Monty Blue of Baytor ex Baytor Lucille (daughter of Ch. Baytor Sasha), bred and owned by Mrs. Anita Westlake, Baytor Kennels, Teignmouth, Devon, England.

three Chow Chows who became progenitors of three separate winning lines of their own, so dominant that they are still in existence even to the time this book is written. These were two dogs and a bitch, Champion Hildewell Ba Tang, Champion Lemning, and Champion Pei Woong of Amwell.

Mr. William Scriven was among those re-entering Chow Chow competition following World War I, his Mulfras dogs making impressive records from about 1920.

The Chow Chow as a breed has flourished in England, with many famous and outstanding dogs having made history there from the early 1920's onward. So complete a coverage from then until the early 1970's has been given in another T.F.H. book on the breed, *The Book of the Chow Chow*, by Dr. Samuel Draper and Joan Brearley, that for us to attempt to chronicle them individually would be superfluous. Everyone interested in this breed should have this excellent book on hand, as it is a treasury of detailed historical information which any one involved with this breed cannot afford to be without.

Baytor Blue Cobweb, a Challenge Certificate winning granddaughter of Champion Baytor Sasha. Anita Westlake, owner, Baytor Kennels, Teignmouth, Devon, England.

At the present time, in the early 1980's, we find no shortage of splendid Chow Chows winning well at British dog shows. Among them are those from the Baytor Kennels, owned by Anita Westlake at Teignmouth in Devon.

The Baytor dogs have met with success both in Great Britain and at shows in Europe. An outstanding dog of inestimable value to this kennel has been the late Baytor Rajah Kuan, whose noted progeny include five champions of exceptional merit. These are Champion Baytor Secret Love, Champion Baytor Sasha, Champion Baytor Choo Choo, Champion Baytor Apricot Silk, and Champion Baytor The Joyful.

Champion Baytor Sasha is the sire of the exciting bitch, Champion Baytor Flossie Flump, who won the highest number of Challenge Certificates of any Chow in England during 1981, to which she added two in 1982 despite very limited showing that year. Sasha is also the grandsire of Champion Baytor Blue Star and Baytor Blue Cobweb, Challenge Certificate-winning litter-sisters, both dams of winning progeny. Other Sasha daughters, including Baytor Moonbeam On The Lake

21

and Baytor Twilight Madonna, have been making their presence felt in keenest competition, too.

Other bitches owned by Mrs. Westlake include Champion Baytor Apricot Silk, Champion Baytor Secret Love, Baytor Blue Enchantress (two Challenge Certificates), and Baytor Special Angel (Reserve Challenge Certificates).

Backing up Sasha among the males are Champion Baytor Choo Choo, Champion Baytor Scarlet Jade, Baytor Gala Performance (Challenge Certificate and Reserve Challenge Certificate winner), and Minhow Monty-Blue of Baytor, the sire of Cobweb and Blue Star.

Then there is the lovely bitch Baytor Sweet Gypsy Rose, the dam of Champion Baytor Scarlet Jade, Baytor Blue Gunsmoke, and Portuguese Champion Baytor Sunset Sue, who has some splendid wins to her credit.

Mrs. Westlake's young daughter, Jenny Westlake, shares her enthusiasm for Chows, and it is she who always handles Moonbeam and Cobweb. As of mid-1983, there are seven Chow champions in this kennel, which has owned more than fifteen in this breed.

Sherivale Chow Chows, owned by Mrs. Iris Bowker and located at Bradford, have been winning well since their beginning back in 1966 when Mrs. Bowker acquired her first of the breed, a black bitch named Minhow Miss Muf Tee. This bitch produced, in her very first litter, Ling of Sherivale, who became the sire of International and Nordic Champion Lord Julian of Sherivale, winner of numerous championship Best in Show awards. Julian distinguished himself by becoming the top Swedish Chow Chow and also proved his value as a sire with his excellent son Champion Sherivale Harlem Lad, bred by Mrs. Bowker and owned by Mrs. Buckley.

It was Cindylu of Briercliffe who won for Mrs. Bowker her first Challenge Certificate and who later became her first champion. This bitch was one of a famous litter bred by Mrs. Cunliffe which included three champions, the others being Champion Russ Kandy of Briercliffe and Champion Brensteven of Briercliffe. The trio was sired by Oranda's A San ex Wendy Lula Ling.

Then came Champion Weircroft Miss Jessica, Best of Breed at Crufts in 1974. Mrs. Ivy Bancroft was her breeder, and she was by Champion Weircroft Venture Boy ex Paula of Weircroft. It was Mrs. Bancroft who also bred Mrs. Bowker's third champion, Weircroft Miss Caroline, another daughter of Venture Boy, this one from Weircroft Precious Gift.

Sherivale Suzanne at eight weeks of age. A young hopeful for the future at Sherivale Kennels, Mrs. Iris Bowker, Bradford, England.

Champion Tamwong Tara was next to follow, bred by Bert and Greta Jones, a daughter of Minhow Masterpiece from Karokaro Rosalind. Still another bitch to become a champion for Mrs. Bowker before she finished her first male was Champion Ranee of Sherivale, by Champion Minhow Many Moons from Ming Wing Loum, bred by J. Harrison.

The first male to gain the title at Sherivale was Champion Smokie Blue Satine of Sherivale, by Justin of Sherivale ex Sherivale's Black Satine. He was bred by Mr. P. Yates.

The future looks bright for this impressive kennel as one contemplates such exciting youngsters as Bobbie Shafton of Sherivale with a Challenge Certificate and three Reserves already to his credit by mid-1983, plus numerous Best in Show awards and, most thrilling of all, Best Dog at the Chow Chow of the Year Show for 1983, with 107 dogs entered. Mrs. Millitt is the breeder of this splendid youngster. Soomer Max was the sire, and Ty-Mo-Shan Amanda the dam.

Then there is Sherivale Tarquin, a homebred by Perky Russ of Nagar ex Sherivale Princess Ria, from every indication another likely future winner.

Dr. Samuel Draper with one of his earliest Chows, Ch. Dre Don Sun King of Craglinden, at Bronx County in March 1967.

24

Chapter 3

Early History in the United States

The popularity of Chow Chows in the United States would seem to have started simultaneously (or soon after) with their recognition in Great Britain; or perhaps they were even a bit earlier in reaching the show ring in the United States since one was recorded as winning third in the Miscellaneous Class at the Westminster Kennel Club event all the way back in 1890. This dog, listed in the catalogue as a "Chinese Chow Chow Dog," belonged to Miss A.C. Derby and was named Takya.

First Champion

The first United States Chow championship was earned by Chinese Chum, imported and owned by Mrs. Charles E. Proctor who maintained the Blue Dragon Kennels. This notable event occurred in June 1905. Adding to his prestige, Chinese Chum became the first Chow champion in the United States to sire a champion when his son, Night of Asia, gained the title the following September. Chinese Chum was evidently a dog of tremendous quality. He gained Best of Breed in keen competition at Westminster in 1906 and served the breed well through his progeny which included, in addition to the aforementioned Champion Night of Asia, another splendid dog, Champion Black Cloud.

Chinese Chum himself was a son of the English Champion Shylock, whom our readers will recall from our British chapter as having been the sire of Mrs. Scaramanga's English Champion Red Craze; and when eventually exported to the United States, he left at least several English champions behind him to help perpetuate his line. Both Shylock and Chinese Chum played important roles in the early American history of the Chow Chow.

The magnificent Ch. Tally's Ho's Black Image of Storm, Best in Show winner of the late 1930's, bred and owned by Tally Ho Kennels, Mrs. Leonard W. Bonney, Oyster Bay, New York.

Early Kennels

Those highly respected Philadelphia fanciers, Dr. and Mrs. Henry Jarrett, were noted for their love of Chows and were among the folks who participated in the founding of the Chow Chow Club, the parent club for the breed in the United States, back in 1906. Dr. Jarrett served as secretary of this organization during its first thirty-five years. A Chow Chow belonging to the Jarretts, Yen How, was a successful early winner at the very beginning of the 1900's. The Jarretts were pioneer fanciers who retained a lifetime interest in their breed.

Mr. Gaston Valcourt, Mandarin Kennels, La Crescenta, California, owned this handsome dog, Int. Ch. Chia-Wan's Black Knight, a popular choice with the judges during the 1940's period.

De Lamar Queen of Hong Kong, a typical and quality bitch of the late 1930's to early 1940's was owned by the Misses Patten of San Fernando, California.

Ch. Wulee Brilliantine
was a highly successful
winner on the Pacific
Coast during the late
1930's to early 1940's
period. Mr. and Mrs.
Cecil Maibach, owners.

One of the most prestigious early kennels was Winsum, owned by Franklin Hutton, where some truly glorious early Chows were imported and raised. Among the most notable of these was Champion Winsum Min T'Sing, born in 1911; we have read many quoted opinions of famous Chowists naming him as the greatest of his day. A son of English Champion Ackum ex Boni, he was sold by Mr. Hutton to Mr. and Mrs. E.C. Waller in 1915. Among this dog's contributions to the breed was a famous and dominant son, Champion Sum Sultan, who was behind some of the famous Ledgelands Chows and Mrs. Prinz's El Cher dogs through Champion Ledgelands' Sancho and Champion Yuan Chu of El Cher respectively.

The foundation of the Ledgelands Kennels, around 1918, was of particular note. Originally these Chow Chows were co-owned by Mr. and Mrs. David Wagstaff of Tuxedo Park, New York, with Harry T. Peters, whose Windholme Beagles and Greyhounds are among the most important in the history of their breeds; the Chows were housed at Mr. Peters's kennel in Islip, Long Island. Mr. Peters's interest in the Chows was not of long duration, however, and the Wagstaffs soon had their dogs installed at their home-kennel in Tuxedo Park, where they remained active until Mrs. Wagstaff's death in the late 1950's. Ralph Hellum was kennel manager here over a very long period of time.

In 1920 Mrs. Wagstaff purchased Kiyodai, a young daughter of English Champion Chelsea Pensioner, who became one of her most valuable foundation bitches. Bred to Champion Sum Sultan, Kiyodai produced Champion Ledgelands Sancho, one of the earliest Ledgelands dogs to finish. Bred to Champion Winsum Min T'Sing, she produced the lovely bitch Ledgelands Busy Issy.

Ledgelands Ula of Sheen was imported from England by Mrs. Wagstaff during this early period, bringing to Ledgelands the bloodlines from Amwell, Lady Faudel Phillips's respected kennel, as her Pusa of Amwell was the sire and the dam was the widely admired English Champion Pickles.

Throughout the 1930's and 1940's Ledgelands campaigned a whole series of successful Chow Chows. The last dog from here was in competition during the 1950's, an importation, Champion Wupei Nagyar Tut, a consistent winner with an impressive record including Bests in Show.

It was during the early 1900's that Mrs. E.K. Lincoln's Greenacre Chows first appeared at her kennel located at Fairfield, Connecticut. Memorable among her dogs was Champion Eastern Star, Best of Breed at Westminster in 1914; Champion Greenacre Tsu Sima; Champion Blue Periwinkle of Kang Shi, imported, and a Best in Show winner in the United States; Champion Greenacre Ah Ling, homebred, Best of Breed at Westminster in 1929; and an impressive number of others. We understand that the total number of champions at this kennel during its lifetime may well have reached at least 50.

Ch. Prince of Pagemoor, son of Ch. Yang Fu Tang, a typical example of the Chow Chows at Pagemoor Kennels, owned by Mr. and Mrs. Frederick Humpage back in the 1930's.

In May 1949 Mrs. Walter Hanson was pictured handling her homebred Ch. Hanson's Hooper Du to Best of Breed at Beverly Riviera K.C. Hooper went on to third in the Group that day.

Best in Show, Ventura 1949. The blue Chow Chow dog, Ch. Blue Blazer of Poppyland owned by Mr. and Mrs. L. Howard Kendall, handled by the latter.

In the early 1920's, Claire Knapp Penney founded the Clairedale Kennels which was to become one of the most influential and famous in the entire American dog fancy. Mrs. Penney, later Mrs. Claire Knapp Dixon, raised many breeds of dogs at various times and had some of the greatest. Her daughter, Margaret P. Newcombe, has followed in her mother's footsteps; and her Pennydale Kennels, although primarily concerned with Whippets, eventually also went into Chows, with very notable results, as we shall describe later.

Probably the greatest of the early Clairedale Chows was their Champion Winsum Min T'Sing son, Champion Clairedale Son Too, who might be described as the beginning of an outstanding Chow-producing dynasty. He sired Champion Far Land Thundergust, who in turn sired Champion Far Land Thunderstorm owned by Mrs. Bonney. Thunderstorm became the sire of Champion Tally Ho Black Image of Storm (Best in Show winner) who carried on the line as the sire of Miss Kathleen Staples's famous and beloved Champion Jimmee Boy.

When Flora (Mrs. Leonard W.) Bonney acquired her first Chow Chow (two of them in fact) from Clairedale Kennels in 1924, she already had been prominent since 1911 as a fancier of Dalmatians and had purchased her first Poodle in 1912. Flora Bonney's impact on all three of these breeds, and on the dog show world in general as a very talented, knowledgeable and highly respected multi-breed judge, goes far beyond words. With her friend and partner, Miss Kathleen Staples, she was active in all aspects of the fancy, and these two ladies each exhibited many memorable dogs and officiated at prestigious dog shows from coast to coast.

The Chow puppies purchased by Mrs. Bonney from Mrs. Penney were Soom of Clairedale and Tally Ho Sultan's Ana. Tally Ho soon became a dominant force in Chows as Mrs. Bonney's interest in the breed expanded. Famous dogs owned by her included Champion Far Land Thunderstorm, purchased from the William MacFarlands in 1932, and his widely admired son, Champion Tally Ho Black Image of Storm, an important Best in Show winner of the 1940's. Then came Champion Jimmee Boy, owned and bred by Kathleen Staples but from the Tally Ho dogs. All of these were truly *great* Chows, recalled with admiration.

Many outstanding dogs during the days previous to the mid-1900's helped to shape the destiny of the Chow Chow in the United States. One of these was Champion Yang Fu Tang, who held the top show-record for the breed until it was broken by Champion Ah Sid the

Dilettante in 1964. Yang Fu Tang was born in 1929 and reached only seven years of age. Yet in that time he amassed the amazing total of 22 Bests in Show (all-breed). He was a son of Champion Yang Fu King ex Yang Fu Queenie, bred by the Hoffmans, Yang Fu Kennels, Milwaukee, Wisconsin, and owned for most of his lifetime by Mrs. Louise Seamer.

Yang Fu Tang was the grandson of the very influential dog, English and American Champion Choonan Brilliantine of Manchoover, who was imported by Mrs. Earl Hoover from his English breeder, Mrs. Manooch. The price paid for Brilliantine is said to have been astronomical, but it would seem to have been well worth it considering his contributions to the breed! Mrs. Hoover had a very respected kennel

Ledgeland Kennels, owned by Mr. and Mrs. David Wagstaff of Tuxedo Park, New York, were dominant in Chows over many years in Eastern competition. Here is one of their "stars," Ch. Wupei Nagyar Tut, with which they did good winning in the mid-1950's. Ralph Hellum, kennel manager, handling.

Elsie Frederick of Strongsville, Ohio, owned and bred this mid-1950's winner, Ch. Independence of Hi Clear, by Ch. Kid Holiday ex Charmar Twinkles So.

of Chows, which included the imported bitch Champion Blue Stocking of Manchoover, first all-breed Best in Show Chow bitch in the United States (Illinois State Fair, August 1929) which no other Chow bitch accomplished until Dr. Imogene Earle's Champion Pandee's Red Sing did so 32 years later!

International Champion Chia Wan's Blue Monarch was another Best in Show winning son of Brilliantine and the sire of noted champions for Mr. and Mrs. Ralph W. Spike, Port Huron, Michigan.

Other greats from the early days include Champion Jo Jo Hanson, Mr. and Mrs. Walter Hanson's fantastic sire and Best in Show dog, whose progeny piled up many big wins during the 1940's and later. Champion East is West and Champion Sun of East, father and son, owned by O.H. West, made their contribution in California late in the 1930's.

Ch. Ah Sid The Aide de Kamp, owned by Dr. William Fritz, handled by Jane Forsyth to Best Non-Sporting Dog, South Shore Kennel Club, 1965.

As the 1930's drew to a close, the Westminster Kennel Club event of 1937 attracted Chow Chow competition which seems to us of special interest for several reasons. More than 40 of the breed were assembled for the opinion of Mrs. A.F. Messmore. The names of many of these dogs, their owners, and the classes in which they were entered has attracted our attention and we wish to share comment on it with you.

This was in the days before Westminster had become "a champions' show" with the number of Specials on hand dominating the entry. Also, puppies had not been eliminated at that time. Obviously, too, exhibitors in those days believed in using all of the classes, not just Open and Specials in entering their dogs, a custom which I would like to see return to popularity. On this occasion, Kathleen Staples had her future star who was to become a formidable champion, Jimmee Boy, entered in the Puppy Class and in Limit (the latter a class which has been eliminated now in favor of Bred-by-Exhibitor), while Mrs. Bonney had another future celebrity, Tally Ho Black Image of Storm, in Novice and in Open Dogs. A thought-provoking commentary on the changes of exhibitor attitude through the years, from then, when winning your class and a blue ribbon was considered fun even by top-flight breeders with fantastically splendid dogs, to now where even the newest exhibitor just starting out is interested only in the points or Best of Breed.

The only Special at Westminster in 1937 was Mrs. Waldo J. Marra's Champion East is West. Champion Far Land Thundergust and his son Champion Far Land Thunderstorm were competing rivals in the Stud Dog Class, each with two of his progeny. Well-known Chowists noted among the exhibitors, in addition to those already mentioned, included the David Wagstaffs, Herold M. Harter, Jr., Mrs. Anny Prinz, O.B. Ziegler, Mrs. William L. Fitzgerald, Greenacre Kennels, Mrs. Howard Emerson, Mrs. Marvin Preston, Mrs. Edward H. Goodwin, Marie Bechtold, Jane Huston, R.B. Koon, Mrs. Emma Clark, and several others.

Chow Chow interest and activity has been constant and on a wide scale in all sections of the United States. It can never be said that good Chows are indigenous to any particular section or area, as this simply is not true. From border to border, coast to coast, Chows of quality and merit have made their contribution to this distinguished breed. We wish that space permitted us to pay tribute here to each and every one of them!

Ch. Ah Sid's The Dilettante with his breeder, Joan Wellborn. Judge, another famous Chow breeder, Mrs. Agrippina Anderson, Glenmont Kennels.

Ch. Five Ash Viki Jo going Best in Show at Elm City in 1968. Owned by Ah Sid and Pennyworth Kennels.

Ch. Eastward Liontamer of Elster then owned by Merilyn Bowden making first in the Non-Sporting Group at Beverly Hills in 1967, prior to coming East under the ownership of Mr. and Mrs. Robert Hetherington and Dr. Samuel Draper. Sired by Ch. Starcrest Spy of Poppyland ex Ken Wan's Tahg Along.

We recently have run across a review of the Chow Chow entry at an important California all-breed dog show of 1940, the winter show of the Los Angeles Kennel Club, which has been hailed as "the Westminster of the Pacific Coast" by fanciers of that period. Mrs. Bonney was the Chow judge, and (considering that it was not a Specialty) the amazing total of sixty Chows were on hand to be evaluated by her, including practically every important dog of this breed on the Pacific Coast. When the smoke of battle had cleared, Canadian and American Champion Chia Wan's Black Knight had emerged the victor; this son of Canadian and American Champion Chia Wan's Red Monarch was owned by Mandarin Kennels and was bred by Mrs. Ralph Spike. Best of Opposite Sex was Champion Honee of Poppyland, sired by Champion Chia Wan's Blue Bedouin, a homebred belonging to Mr. and Mrs. L.H. Kendall. Thus we have an idea of who and what was winning on the Pacific Coast as well as in the East as we went from the 1930's into the 1940's.

Mr. and Mrs. Ralph W. Spike of Port Huron, Michigan, were, as the record shows, important Chow Chow breeders back then and in later times.

As for the Howard Kendalls, of Poppyland fame, right from the acquisition of their first Chow Chow, The Pagoda King, in the 1930's, they have been high on the lists of outstanding fanciers. Champion Honee of Poppyland was their first big-winning homebred, starting her ring career with Best in Non-Sporting Group at an important show. Probably "pride of place" among the Poppyland dogs must go to Champion Starcrest Spy of Poppyland, bred by Joel Marston, from Poppyland Choo Choo by the famous Champion Ghat de la Moulaine. This worthy winner goes down in history as the sire of the founder of the Liontamer Dynasty, Champion Eastward Liontamer of Elster.

The first of the many champions owned by the Howard Kendalls was Champion Tonkee Brilliantine.

In the East, I recall with admiration the dogs owned by several fanciers of whom we have not yet written. My good friends John and Agrippina Anderson at Silver Spring, Maryland, owned an especially impressive dog in their gorgeous Champion Dai Fu King of Glenmont, who was a big winner during the 1940's. These were very delightful and energetic people who loved all phases of the dog show world and were instrumental in founding at least several of the all-breed kennel clubs in the Washington, D.C. area. Another important contribution they made was in encouraging their friend Joan

This early 1960's Best in Show winning Chow Chow is Ch. Loy Jean's China Boi. Owned by Loy-Jean Kennels, Floyd and Jean Messer, Redmond, Washington.

Ch. Scotchow Liontamer's Louise at eight and a half months winning Best Non-Sporting Dog at Huntington Kennel Club in May 1968. This Chow had a win-filled career for owner Joan Hannephin and handler Nancy Lenfesty. Sired by Ch. Eastward Liontamer of Elster ex Ch. Scotchow Sing A Long.

Wellborn's interest in breeding Chows, as we are certain that their support and enthusiasm had much to do with Joan's phenomenal success as a Chow breeder, and with her unforgettable dog, Champion Ah Sid's the Dilettante.

In New England were George and Nina Armitage, whom I recall as exhibitors back in the 1930's, bringing sizeable entries of very good Chows to many of the Connecticut and Massachusetts shows. Also Mr. and Mrs. Frederic P. Humpage of Pagemoor fame, from whom Joan Wellborn purchased one of her earliest winners, Champion Pagemoor's Son of Wag-gee, a dog she admired for his outstanding balance; he became the grandsire of her incomparable "Buddy," Champion Ah Sid's the Dilettante.

Chang-Shi Kennels were established in the mid-1940's by Jerry and Lucille Sterling, based on imported dogs from Germany and Belgium. The Sterlings, who are from Nashville, Tennessee, established an exciting record for Chows when, in 1957, they scored a world's record in

Ch. Dusten's Talcum Powder takes a 3-point major earning the title. By Ky-Lin Dusten's Pink Dude ex Ky-Lin Powder Power. Bred and owned by Dusten and John Cox, Sharon, Connecticut.

40

Ch. Cherokee's Red Feather, a most beautiful and typical example of the Chow Chows winning during the late 1960's. One of the lovely dogs from Cherokee Kennels, Mr. and Mrs. E. Crisp, Cathlamet, Washington.

the breed, campaigning five homebred littermates to championship—all by the time they had reached ten months of age! As frosting on the cake, two of the males along the way became Group winners.

Many of you will find the Charmar Chows behind your present winners. Mrs. Charles Evans began breeding in 1939, a line-breeding program based on Charmar Ching, C.D. A collection of excellent bitches was assembled specifically for breeding to this dog, carrying the bloodlines of the leading champions of that era. The result has been a splendid and predictable strain, reliable to work with and highly satisfactory in every respect. One has but to note the large number of Charmar champions, and winners descended from them, to admire the success of Mrs. Evans's breeding theories!

Florence Wilson Graham since the early 1920's was in love with the Chow Chow. Her first members of the breed came from Mr. Mac-Monnies, Snoo Kee II (who was a daughter of Champion Maxown Punch) and Snoo Kee's litter sired by Champion Su Tsun of Five Ash, the stud Mrs. Graham selected for her, owned by Mrs. Lincoln. One of the puppies, Su Tsun of Five Ash II, grew up to become a famous and widely admired champion, the first to gain the title for Mrs. Graham and her foundation sire.

Champion Five Ash Jo Jo, by the great Champion Jo Jo Hanson ex Five Ash Gloming, was acquired by Mrs. Graham as a puppy. He became a most famous winner and stud dog. Another son of Champion Jo Jo Hanson was also owned by Mrs. Graham, this one Champion Five Ash Black Magic. Mrs. Graham loved both the red and the

Ch. Lakeview's Han-Sum, Mamie R. Gregory's Best in Show winning Chow Chow, here is handled to the top award at Manatee Kennel Club. Han-Sum's record, a very exciting one, was gained in keenest competition throughout the United States.

black Chow Chows, and her influence on the quality of the black Chows in southern California proved highly beneficial.

Champion Five Ash Jo Jo sired the lovely homebred Champion Five Ash Victory, noted for his quality as a winning show dog and as a sire. Victory in turn, among his numerous winners, produced the fantastic Champion Five Ash Vicki Jo, the Chow so lovely that he brought together a partnership to own him consisting of Joan Wellborn of Ah Sid fame and Margaret P. (Peggy) Newcombe, the daughter of Mrs. Claire Knapp Penney whose Clairedale Chows had been so important several decades before. Vicki Jo, in the late 1960's, came East like a conquering hero to his new owners, to be handled by Jeanne Millet. His success was instantaneous; and his tragic death only far too short a time later was a heartbreak for all who love this breed.

I doubt that Florence Graham herself had an exact count of the number of champion Chows she bred and finished through the years; but there would seem little question that she is far and away the leader in this respect, and we pay tribute to her vast contribution to the Chow Chow in America.

Mrs. Valetta E. Gotschall of Carrollton, Ohio, goes down in the Chow Chow world's hall of fame as the breeder of the beautiful, typical, highly successful Champion Gotschall's Van Van. Born July 2nd 1963, Van Van was by Champion Loy Jean's Chi Yan Kid ex Gotschall's Dusty and was co-owned by Mrs. Gotschall and Donald L. Drennan. Van Van's show career was very noteworthy indeed, including Best in Show honors and, probably the most treasured of all by his owners, the win of Best Non-Sporting Dog at Westminster Kennel Club under that greatly respected judge, Alva Rosenberg.

It was back in 1933 when Mrs. Gotschall's breeding program was established, starting out with the Champion Yang Fu Tang line, later introducing their Champion Ah Lee Hi Tiger on their bitches, and, in the 1960's, the Champion Ghat de la Moulaine line. Van Van and their other Best in Show winner, Champion Gotschall's Chang Kuo Chian, are direct results of this breeding.

Probably about two dozen champions by now have been produced at Gotschall Kennels.

One of the kennels I have noticed most frequently behind current Chows of today in both the United States and Canada is Nor-Ton, owned by Bessie Van Dusen Volkstadt of North Tonawanda, New York. For several decades or longer this lady has been a devoted breeder of Chow Chows, and some of the greats from her kennel include American and Canadian Champion Nor-Ton's Tin Sin, American and Canadian Champion Nor-Ton's Half Moon, Champion Nor-Ton's Silver Moon, and Champion Arrogant Melody of Nor-Ton, to mention just a few.

Naomi Scott Humphries is the lady behind Lakeview Chows at Louisville, Kentucky, where many prestigious winners have been raised. Probably her most exciting litter was that of the destined six future champions, including the renowned Champion Lakeview's Han Sum, produced by Champion Lakeview's Chum of Waulee ex Lakeview's Yum Yum, born July 5th 1964. Han Sum was sold to Mamie Reynolds Gregory after winning the St. Louis Specialty from the classes, and, handled by her husband, Joe Gregory, this lovely dog became a source of much pleasure to Mamie as he racked up a record show career. A partnership was formed in the early 1970's of Naomi Scott Humphries, Davis S. Reynolds, and Don Aull, for the continuation of Lakeview Chow Chows.

One of the most famous names in our modern Chow Chow world is that of Champion Ghat de la Moulaine, a dog who came from France in 1959 when he was twenty months of age to join the distinguished Chows belonging to Clif and Vivian Shyrock at Hawaiian Gardens, California. The impact of this dog on the American Chow Chow world has been tremendous, with his bloodlines to be found in the majority of important breeding kennels here. Progeny of his have followed in their sire's footsteps as great producers and great show dogs right on down through succeeding generations.

Ghat was top winning Chow Chow in the United States for 1960 and fifth ranking dog of all breeds. The following year he was the top Non-Sporting Group stud dog. Sad to say, this great dog met with an early accidental death in 1963. Who can even begin to estimate the extent of this loss to the breed?

Joel Marston's Starcrest Kennels in California is a top one. Tsang Po, founded by Hal and Marie Allen of Lubbock, Texas, back in the early 1940's and continued since 1969 at Jackson, Mississippi, by Dr. and Mrs. Edward North, has made its presence felt over several decades. Mary MacEachern with her Wu Sans carried on an active breeding program at Sodus, New York, and her Bermudian and American Champion Ky-Lin's Midas was a Westminster Best of Breed winner, among other coveted honors. There have been so many, many more dogs and people who have contributed their share to making the Chow Chow the widely admired favorite the breed has become.

A full-face view of the mighty "Buddy." Ch. Ah Sid's the Dilettante, owned by Ah Sid Kennels and handled by Jane Forsyth, taking Best in show at Twin Brooks Kennel Club in 1964.

Southern Chow Chow Club Specialty Show, April 1962, judged by Kenneth Stine had as its winner, Ch. Chum Yong Fu Fun owner-handled by Mrs. Earl L. Humphries. Club President Russell Saul presents the trophy.

Ch. Starcrest Spy of Poppyland at Beverly Hills Kennel Club in 1966. Maxwell Riddle awarding him Best in Show and Carolyn Jones presenting the trophy. Howard Kendall, owner-handler of this magnificent Chow Chow.

Opposite page: Fifteen-month-old Ch. Charmar Sing Song by Ch. Charmar Chatterbox ex Charmar Grand Duchess, completing his title at Skokie Valley Kennel Club, October 1968 under judge William Kendrick. Bred, owned and handled by Mrs. Charles Evans.

The lovely chow, Ch. Five Ash Viki Jo is co-owned by Ah Sid and Pennyworth Kennels. Unfortunately this dog died at an early age while at the height of his show career.

The Chow Chow Club

Everyone who owns a purebred dog really owes it to himself, and to his or her dog, to join a Specialty club devoted to that breed. There are many benefits to be derived from such a membership, including the opportunity to make friends with people who share your mutual interest, to broaden your education about the breed, to attend meetings, to participate in such club activities as match shows, Specialty shows and training classes, and to win the honors and awards bestowed by the majority of clubs to be competed for by their members.

The National Specialty club for Chows, the breed's parent club, is the Chow Chow Club Incorporated, a member of the American Kennel Club, founded in 1906. This club holds an annual Specialty show, each year in a different region of the United States, these events drawing a hundred or more Chows each time to compete for wins considered to be the most prestigious attainable in the breed during that year. The annual meeting of the membership is held in conjunction with the annual Specialty show, making it a very important occasion for Chow Chow lovers. The dates are usually in the spring, and an effort is made to include featured events such as educational seminars as part of the accompanying activities.

If you are interested in joining the Chow Chow Club, you will need the sponsorship of a member with whom you are already acquainted. Very likely the breeder of your puppy or grown dog would come under this heading and would be glad to sponsor you. Or if you are already attending dog shows, you may very well have met members of the parent club in this manner who would be not only willing but happy to sponsor you.

In addition to the parent club, there are numerous regional Specialty clubs in this breed, each covering a specific area. When you purchase your Chow, inquire of the breeder as to whether or not there is one covering your locality, and if so, immediately contact the secretary, telling of your interest, that you would like to join, and ask if you may attend a meeting (or if there is a match show or other activity coming up) in order to become acquainted with the members—and vice versa. Once having joined a regional club, you will make friends and it should be quite easy from that point to get one to sponsor you for the parent club. Membership applicants are published in *Chow Life*, the parent club's quarterly magazine; ballots on new members are sent to the Board of Directors for voting 45 days after the names are published, and twenty days are allowed for the marked ballots to be returned, bringing the entire process to several months before your approval is received. In the regional clubs it is a faster process. Most Chow Chow fanciers like to belong to a regional club and to the parent club.

Annual dues for membership in the Chow Chow Club are $10 per person, plus $15 for a subscription to *Chow Life*. This magazine, by the way, is also available to non-members at $18 per year and is one of the best investments any Chow owner can make. Each issue is chock-full of educational material, valuable articles on the breed, photographs of current winners, and advertising telling where good Chows are available for sale. At the time of this writing, subscriptions are available through Mrs. Carol Patterson, 19180 Rising Sun Road, Corona, CA 91720. Members of the Chow Chow Club are required to obey the rules of the American Kennel Club, the club's by-laws, and to adhere to the Chow Chow Club's Code of Ethics.

The Chow Chow Club's recording secretary is Mrs. Andrea Moore, 866 Newtown Road, Martsons Mills, MA 02648, from whom membership applications can be obtained.

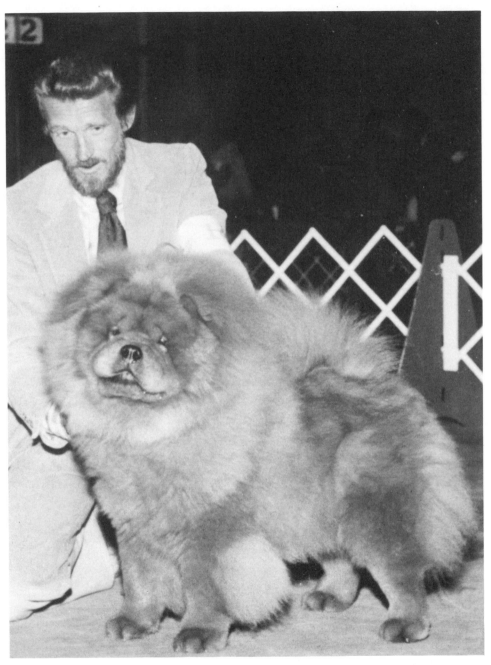

Ch. Shanghai's Mastradomas, by Ch. Laral's Excalibur by Weiss ex Cedar Creek's Miss Muffet at seven months old. Breeder, K. Jane Weiss. Owners, AHSO Fan-C Chows, Les and Marilyn Short, Wichita, Kansas.

Chapter 4

Kennels in the United States

AHSO FAN-C

AHSO Fan-C Chow Chows belong to Les and Marilyn Short, formerly of Belle Plains, Kansas, who will be settled at their new home and kennel in Wichita by the time you are reading this book.

Marilyn Short had her first Chow Chow when she was only five years old. As she says, "within the 50 years which followed there have been many Chowlets enriching our lives and creating our Chowmania, indelibly guiding our hobby of breeding and loving Chow Chows." For many years, the Shorts have bred Chows for companion dogs and pets, but they were not then yet interested in showing. Les Short was a professional pilot. In 1978 he had by-pass surgery on his heart, which ended his career in flying. Something was needed to fill the void when it was necessary to sell Les's airplane and to give the Shorts something new in which to involve themselves. So it was decided to breed their best champion-sired Chow bitch, Red Penny, to the best current champion stud dog they could locate. When they saw Champion Rhythm Special Delivery, bred by Victoria Helferich and owned by Ed and Debbie Cunningham, both Shorts instantly agreed that the long search had ended! This sound and beautiful dog is sired by Champion Melody's Rustic Masterpiece, who was Number One Chow Chow, Phillips System, at the time.

The results of this breeding gave the Shorts their first champion-quality puppy, who grew up to become Champion AHSO Big Rock Candy Mountain. At five months of age, he was Best in Match at Ponca City, Oklahoma, Kennel Club. At six months he was Best in Sweepstakes, North Texas Chow Chow Club Specialty, where his littermate, AHSO Topaz Trophy, was Best of Opposite Sex. From there he took seven consecutive Bests of Breed awards over Specials, finishing

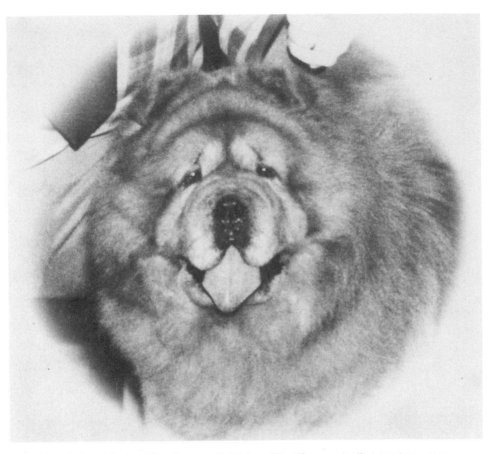

A lovely headstudy of Ch. Pinewoods Hickory Dic, "Comanche," at age two years. By Ch. Pinewood's Renaissance ex Brandy Kwong Chow. Breeders, Charles and Pamela Estip. Owners, Les and Marilyn Short.

his title at eight months of age from Puppy Classes. At seven months he had taken his first Group placement, a third from the Puppy Class under judge Robert Wills.

Rocky has made a good mark for himself as a stud dog, too, with his first two litters. Three from the first litter are pointed, of which AHSO's Rock A Bye Baby, owned by Dewain and Brenda Garrolts, of Nebraska, should be finished by now.

In 1982 the Shorts purchased Pinewood's Hickory Dic, known as "Comanche," finishing him in three and a half weeks. He was bred by Charles and Pamela Estep and is sired by Champion Pinewood's Renaissance, who was Number Two Chow Chow in the United States

AHSO Fan-C War Drummer, ASHI, by Ch. Pinewoods Hickory Dic ex AHSO Topaz Trophy O'Prophet, was Best of Breed at both Spartenburg and Ashville Kennel Clubs for 3-point majors both days, judged by Mrs. Vandeventer and Dr. Draper respectively. Owned by Anne A. and Ashley A. Hampton, handled by Norm Hampton.

At three months of age, AHSO Fan-C Ruffles N' Flourishes already shows promise of the beautiful dog into which he has matured.

in mid-1983. He took top honors at the 1983 Chow Chow Club Specialty and is a multiple all-breed Best in Show winner. Comanche has proven a valuable addition to the Shorts' Chow family, a red dog of dignity and beauty. AHSO Topaz Trophy was bred to Comanche, producing lovely quality puppies, some of which are now in competition. One of these is AHSO Fan-C Comanche Warbonnet, owned by the Shorts and ready to start her show career in late 1983. From the same litter, AHSO Comanche War-Dancer Ahashi, owned by Anne and Ashley Hampton of Lewisburg, West Virginia, already has points on her title, which is nearing completion.

During the spring of 1983, the Shorts finished their red male puppy, Shanghai Mastradomas of AHSO, within 30 days of his first show. This one was bred by K. Jane Weiss at Pottsville, Pennsylvania (Shanghai Chows), and is sired by Champion Laral's Excalibur by Weiss from Cedar Creek's Miss Muffet. This newest champion will be Specialed in the fall of 1983, and the Shorts are eagerly anticipating a

AHSO Fan-C Ruffles N' Flourishes in April 1983, age six months, with his breeder-owner Marilyn Short. By Ch. AHSO Big Rock Candy Mountain ex Jade. AHSO Fan-C Chow Chows, Les and Marilyn Short.

Two cinnamons, three-month-old littermates: *left,* AHSO Fan-C Pomp N' Circumstances; *right,* AHSO Fan-C Ruffles N' Flourishes, by Ch. AHSO Big Rock Candy Mountain ex Jade. Les and Marilyn Short, owners.

Ch. AHSO Big Rock Candy Mountain, the first Chow exhibited by the Shorts, and their first homebred champion, by Ch. Rhythm Special Delivery ex Red Penny winning the breed here from the classes at age seven months. Breeder-owners, Les and Marilyn Short.

litter by him from their cinnamon girl, Jade, who in 1982 produced three very exceptional puppies by AHSO Fan-C Ruffles N' Flourishes, all of them cinnamon like their dam. AHSO Fan-C Ruffles N' Flourishes took Best in Match when only three months of age at Central California Chow Chow Club Specialty Match under noted Chow breeder-judge Joel Marston.

The Shorts keep their kennel small, numbering usually fewer than twenty Chows. Les will be retiring in 1984, and then they will be traveling with their Chows and showing as much as is possible. This should be fun for them considering the obvious high quality of their dogs. With that thought in mind, a bit more breeding than usual is taking place at the kennel so that the Shorts will have some super youngsters ready to start out when they are.

The Shorts enjoy handling their own dogs, and it is only if the show is on a date inconvenient for Les that a handler takes over. Then it is John Roberts who takes the dogs, doing a splendid job with them.

Al De Bear

Al De Bear Chow Chows are owned by Alan and Delores Stamm and are located at Jacksonville, Florida. The first and founding Chow dog here was Champion Satchmo De Blackbear Kid, purchased by the Stamms at the age of seven months. He was a black son of the outstanding blue, Champion Starcrest Periwinkle.

Satchmo turned out to be the ideal dog for the novice owner. He was a winner to stimulate their enthusiasm but not a "flyer" going through too quickly; thus the Stamms had the opportunity to show often. The Stamms say of him, "He was always the perfect gentleman in the ring, but didn't show himself, thus he made us work to learn to show." Additionally, Satchmo proved to be a producer of offspring even better than himself, producing beautiful sound and typey dogs.

The Stamms' next purchase was a blue bitch who became Champion Tiawin Tangled Up 'N Blue. Tang was acquired at eleven months of age; and after a litter, when the Stamms took her out to the shows, she finished in three weekends. Her mother was Starcrest Heather of

Al De Bear Sweet 'N Low, by Ch. Heritage Jean Lafitte ex Al De Bear Black Velvet, lovely winning bitch bred and owned by Alan and Deloris Stamm, Jacksonville, Florida.

Al De Bear Ambrosia, with ten points including three majors, is by Ch. Al De Bear Snickers ex Mar Car Sing Mi Soong. Alan and Deloris Stamm, breeder-owners, Jacksonville, Florida.

Opposite page: Ch. Al De Bear Kodiak, by Ch. Al De Bear Hustler ex Al De Bear Sweet N' Low, bred and owned by Alan and Deloris Stamm, Jacksonville, Florida.

WINNERS

...VILLE DOG
...S ASSOC INC
JAN 1983

Al De Bear Almond Joy is a cinnamon bitch by Ch. Heritage Jean Lafitte ex Al De Bear Elsa. Another fine homebred owned by Alan and Deloris Stamm.

Tiawin, who was a full sister to Satchmo's sire. Satchmo and Tang were both heavily bred to the Starcrest lines, and this was the foundation on which Al De Bear has been built.

Two of the blue offspring from the Satchmo-Tang breeding were Starcrest Blue Stocking and Champion Al De Bear Sox Up Starcrest. The latter dog, Sox, was a winner on both the East Coast and on the West Coast, shown by the Stamms in the East and by Joel Marston of Starcrest Kennels on the West Coast. Sox has also proven himself an excellent producer, with such offspring to his credit as the black bitch Champion Al De Bear Lace Galaxie who won a Group placement at six months of age, handled by her owner (a novice at the time), and Champion Al De Bear Hustler, who was Number Eight in the nation, based on number of Chows defeated, in 1981, with limited showing and from the Puppy Class! Most recently another black Sox daughter, Al De Bear Black Lady, has gone Best in Show in Peru as a puppy.

The Stamms have owned, bred, and sold fifteen champions, and during the past five years they have had ten homebred champions. They have always made it a point to sell *good* dogs to new people joining the fancy and are proud of the fact that all the Al De Bear champions have been, to date, owned and finished personally by their owners.

Cabaret

Cabaret Chow Chows are owned by the Richard family, Joan and James Richard and their daughter Jamie, and are located at Bay City, Michigan.

It is Jamie Richard who has replied to my inquiry about the Chows and about her success as a junior handler. She tells us that she received her first show dog as a gift from her parents and that it was with this dog, who became Champion Cabaret Blackjack, C.D., that she became actively interested in dog shows and in obedience. She handled "Muggsy" to his title, at the same time herself competing in the Novice Classes of Junior Showmanship. "Muggsy" attained his C.D. title in three consecutive shows and also won his conformation championship. And that was the beginning of Jamie Richard's life with dog shows.

In 1981, Jamie was determined to try to gain the eight first-place wins in Junior Showmanship which would qualify her to compete at Westminster. She began showing her parents' magnificent homebred Champion Cabaret Joker in Junior and had been doing so for about a month when she decided to try Specialing him. Their first time in the Group ring, Jamie and Joker took first place. Jamie then continued both to Special Joker and to work for those Junior Showmanship awards. In late November she received her eighth first place in Junior Showmanship, thus becoming eligible to compete at Westminster in 1982.

Jamie's New Year's resolution for 1982 was to work Joker six times each week in their practice ring in the basement, in preparation for the great event. Her hard work paid off, for when "the Garden" was over, Jamie had become the first junior handler to make the Westminster Junior Showmanship finals with a Chow. Needless to say, there was great happiness in the Richard household and pride for Jamie in knowing that her hard work and determination had paid off.

Two months later Champion Cabaret Joker took his first Best in Show while being handled by Jamie. As Jamie says, "He showed the whole day so superbly, almost as if he knew it was his day."

Joker and Jamie finished out the year with another Best in Show and several Groups and placements, making Joker Number Six Chow in the ratings systems.

College is now in Jamie's plans for the immediate future. But she would not rule out the possibility of someday becoming a professional handler, as she has greatly enjoyed showing dogs and the whole aspect of dog shows.

As for the Cabaret Chows, one has but to note Joker's quality to realize the success with which Joan and James Richard have met as breeders. Born in September 1975, Joker is a son of Champion Fa-Ci Chinkapin ex Champion Audrich Star From The East and is a home-bred in which any breeder would take great pride.

Ch. Cabaret Blackjack completing his title at Detroit Kennel Club, March 1976. Handled by Joan Richard. A son of Ch. Audrich Tuff Stuff ex Ch. Audrich Star from the East, bred and owned by Cabaret Chows.

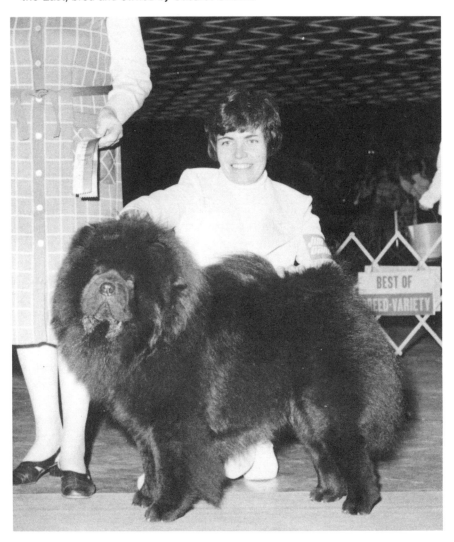

Ch. Cabaret Joker taking his fifth all breed Best in Show under John Connolly at Oakland City Kennel Club, May 23rd 1982, handled by Jamie Richard. A son of Ch. Fa-Ci Chinkapin ex Ch. Audrich Star from the East; bred and owned by Joan and James Richard.

Cedar Creek

Cedar Creek Chows are owned by Frances Speers of Oklahoma City, Oklahoma, who has been breeding them since the mid-1970's.

The sire behind all of the Cedar Creek dogs is Jewell's Super Manchu, a most handsome dog bred by Jewell Cassabury of Houston, Texas.

Champion Cedar Creek's Ginger Cookie has been an especially good producing bitch and is the dam of Champion Kitts Tinks-A-Yantzee and Biddle's Rose of Sharon.

Cedar Creeks Casey Jones is another favorite, as is Cedar Creek's Shawnee.

Ms. Spears is a very enthusiastic Chow breeder who truly enjoys the companionship and beauty of her dogs, who have proven a credit to her for their own quality and as producers.

Cedar Creek's Shawnee at ten months old, winning Best of Winners from Mrs. Walton at Ft. Wayne, Indiana, in 1981. By Super Manchu ex Foon Ying's Don't Ja Loveit. Breeder, Bonnie Henson; owner, Frances Speers.

Cedar Creek's Casey Jones, by Ch. Jonel's Track Two ex Cedar Creek Nubbins O'Frelin was bred by Bonnie Henson and is owned by Frances Speers.

Ch. Kitt's Tinks-A-Yantzee on left, taking a 4-point major. Biddle's Rose of Sharon with 11 points. These littermates by Am. and Can. Ch. Plainacres Yantzee of Kobys ex Ch. Cedar Creek's Ginger Cookie shown here with Sharon Biddle and C. Kitts.

Ch. Dusten's Pink Panther, by Ch. Glen Shiel Porthos ex Ch. Pennyworth Hey Look Me Over, purchased by Justen and John Cox in 1970 was the start of their breeding program. A great-grandson of Ch. Ah Sid's The Dilettante, most of the present day Dusten winners go back to him.

Dusten's

Dusten Cox saw her first Chow Chow while on her way back to the convent boarding school she was then attending in Florida, and from that moment on she wanted one of these gorgeous dogs. Problem was, she ended up married to a man who was afraid of *all* dogs, never mind a Chow. So Dusten and her cats invested in a Christmas Club, the proceeds of which were to be used to purchase the first purebred dog for her husband, John Cox. She purchased not a Chow Chow but a Keeshond. Dusten's reasoning was that if he would learn to love a Kees and overcome his fear of dogs, sooner or later she would be able to have her Chow. One must say that Dusten's plan worked well, for not only did John overcome his fear of dogs, but he also personally handled three Kees to their championships! By now he has a long list of Chow Chows he has finished and with whom he has won prestigious Bests in Show and Group victories as well, for he has turned out to be a most capable handler. Dusten's Chows are located in Sharon, Connecticut.

Dusten and John got their first Chow in 1964, having waited for two years until Joan Wellborn of the famed Ah Sid Kennels was able to come up with a black dog with whom she felt Dusten would be satisfied. He turned out to have been well worth the wait, as he became Champion Ky-Lin's Black Power, by Ah Sid Silver Chalice ex Ky-Lin Orange Blossom, bred by Betty Mae Seward. In speaking of this magnificent Chow, Dusten writes, "I honestly don't think there was ever a dog loved as much as this one. To own our first Chow and be lucky enough to have two Bests in Show on him, owner-handled by Jack, is truly awesome."

It was in 1970, with the arrival of Champion Dusten's Pink Panther, that the Coxes entered into the breeding of Chows. Pink Panther was a great grandson of the noted Champion Ah Sid the Dilettante, and right up until the present time the majority of the Dusten Chows trace back to him.

Ch. Ky-Lin Black Power (Ah Sid Silver Chalice ex Ch. Ky Lin's Orange Blossom) winning one of his Bests in Show, owner-handled, as always, by John Cox for himself and Dusten Cox.

Dusten's Bring-N-Da Bacon, by Dusten's Saturday Nite Fever ex Ky Lin Great Pumpkin at seven months. Just starting out in 1983, in two ring appearances Best of Breed from the classes over specials. Dusten and John Cox, owners. John Cox handling.

Both of these handsome Chow Chows, scoring a double victory under judge Mrs. Inez Hartley, are sired by Ch. Car Mar Pucker for Dusten, owned by John and Dusten Cox.

The Coxes maintain a Chow kennel of about twenty adults, of which several are now Dusten's "geriatrics," plus they usually have four or five "teenagers" standing in the wings getting ready for show careers. By mid-1983 the Coxes have finished around twenty champions, either owned by them or of their breeding. Now into their sixth generation of Pink Panther descendants, their hopes are high for a youngster named Dusten's Bring-n-Da Bacon who looks to have extremely exciting potential. Who knows—he may well develop into a Best in Show winner. It would not be in the least surprising!

Kamara

Kamara Kennels were established in 1971 with the acquisition, by Carl and Marcia Boudreau of Rockland, Massachusetts, of a son of Champion Eastward Liontamer of Elster from American Kennel Club judge Mrs. Sylvia Bonnell. At this time the Boudreaus were also very active in Shetland Sheepdogs, owning several fine winning representatives of this breed.

In 1973 the Boudreaus acquired, from Bob and Jean Hetherington, (co-owners with Dr. Samuel Draper of Liontamer), a handsome young dog, Liontamer Bruiser, also sired by Liontamer, and a bitch sired by Champion Tag-El's Little Rock, known as Nora. They campaigned Bruiser as a Special, and with many fine wins to his credit he became Number Thirteen Chow Chow in 1975. Nora was in the background with her brood of puppies sired by Bruiser.

A dog and a bitch were kept by the Boudreaus from the Nora-Bruiser litter, who grew up to become Champion Kamara Ruby-Foo and Champion Kamara Baby Huey. It was Huey who distinguished himself at the Southern Chow Chow Club Specialty Show in 1975, in conjunction with the National Specialty, as he won the Junior Dog Sweepstakes there that year. Ruby did not do badly, either, winning the Bred-by-Exhibitor Class at that National.

Kamara Sunshine Superman by Dusten Kamara John Boi ex Ch. Kamara Pandora at one and a half years old taking his second major at Camden County in 1978. Breeder-owners, Carl and Marcia Boudreau.

Michael Leavitt of New Hampshire is the proud owner of this most handsome four-month-old baby Chow, Shenandoah of Kamara, a fine representative of the Kamara breeding program carried out by the Boudreaus.

Bruiser proved an exceptional stud dog, siring other top-quality males and females in the years that followed. His name can be found in the pedigrees of many winners, some several times over. His untimely death in 1978 saddened the Boudreaus greatly, and he remains a part of their hearts today as he always will. As Marcia Boudreau writes, "Champion Liontamer Bruiser—we were privileged to have known and loved him."

A gorgeous black son of Bruiser's, Kamara Joy To The World (both majors in a total of ten points) was the winner of a large Open Black Class at the 1979 National Specialty. Throughout the 1970's and thus far in the 1980's, Kamara Chows have made many worthy wins with their various homebreds, both the dogs and the bitches.

A very special dog, one who was lost in 1981 just a single point short of his title, was the gorgeous black Kamara Sunshine Superman, who scored, back-to-back, five-point majors at the prestigious Atlantic City-Camden weekend. A dog of tremendous quality and potential, his death came as a real blow to his owners. His lovely black dam, Kamara Pandora, a Liontamer daughter, lives on, playful as a puppy at nine years of age, ruling the household of her owner, Michael Leavitt, in New Hampshire.

Delta Dawn of Kamara, female, photo at five months. Owned by Geri De Sousa and Carl Boudreau.

The Boudreaus have been adding new blood to their original breeding stock, with very eye-pleasing results. They have found the combination of Bruiser and the Plainacre lines an ideal cross, producing such standout results as the soon-to-become champion Quasi of Kamara and the also close-to-title Jeanette of Kamara, both of whom should be sporting their titles by the time you are reading this.

Latest hopefuls for the show ring include some very impressive youthful Chowlets. Among them are Last Tango of Kamara, Dolly Dawn of Kamara, and Shenandoah of Kamara.

Two new champions during 1982 were Champion Jonel's Track Two of Kamara (a Kemo Kym grandson) and Champion Kamara Molly-O, line-bred from Liontamer.

The Boudreaus are doing a splendid job of accomplishing the goals they have set for themselves as breeders: good hips; clear eyes without loss of head type; sound temperaments—dogs who are making friends for their breed wherever they are known.

Kim-Sha

Kim-Sha Chow Chows, at Oklahoma City, Oklahoma, are a fairly new project, their owner, Barbara Hamon, having acquired her first pet puppy in 1980. Unfortunately, parvo was running rampant at the time, and the pup caught and succumbed to this dread disease.

Heartbroken, but by then in love with the breed, Barbara acquired another from the same breeder, Frances Speers, and became interested in obedience competition. That quickly led to interest in conformation showing, and she bought a show male from Starcrest—Beamer bloodlines, bred by Hewell Casselberry.

This was Jewell's Echo Mingus, which is now the stud dog at Kim-Sha. Mingus's very first son, Kim-Sha's Red Man Chew, took a Best in Match at the age of twelve weeks. Mingus's daughters will be bred to top studs, and their daughters bred back to Mingus. Thus Mrs. Hamon has plans for the future nicely formulated, and we wish her success.

Kim-Sha Kennels are named for Mrs. Hamon's two daughters, *Kim*berly and *Sha*ron.

Three-and-a-half-month-old "Moe" contemplates his ribbon for the day at a recent match show where he was Best Chow puppy and third in Group. Kim-Sha's Red Man Chew owned by Barbara Hamon.

Jewell's Echo Mingus, by Jewell's Oriental Jo-Jo ex Jewell's Cindy Dolly Tiawin. Bred by Jewell Casselberry, owned by Barbara Hamon.

Ky-Lin

For the past thirty years Ky-Lin Chow Chows, owned by Betty-Mae Sewards, have been a dream come true for this talented fancier who first saw the breed as a child in Scotland in the mid-1930's. And certainly this kennel has been one of strong influence and value to the fancy right up to the present day.

Nor-Ton's Yim-Lee, purchased from Bessie Volkstadt, was the foundation dog from whom Ky-Lin has developed. This was a very special dog when one contemplates his achievements. Included among them are a Westminster Best of Breed; American and Canadian championships; and obedience degrees in both the United States and Canada, which is a unique accomplishment within this breed. Ky-Lin Kennels are in Spencerville, Indiana, but Ky-Lin Chow Chows are behind the breed in many parts of the United States and Canada. It would be hard to give an exact figure, but I would guess that the total number of champions bred here, or descended from Ky-Lin dogs, is awe-inspiring, to say the least.

Liontamer

The Liontamer Kennel story has its beginning back in 1967 when Dr. Samuel Draper, who prior to then had owned such outstanding Chows as the magnificent black dog Champion Ah Sid the Avant Garde and Champion Dre-Don Sun-King of Craglinden, and Mr. and Mrs. Robert A. Hetherington, owners of the famous Arrogant Bulldogs at Mahwah, New Jersey, joined forces for the purchase of Champion Eastward Liontamer of Elster from Marilyn Bowden Morgan in California, bringing this great dog East.

Liontamer's success in the East was instantaneous, both as a sire and as a show dog. By the time of his retirement he had been in the Top Ten Chows over a number of years, while in 1969, 1970, and 1971 he was Supreme Chow based on the parent club's rating system. His total show record includes ten Bests in Show all breeds, 52 Non-Sporting Groups, and over three hundred times Best of Breed. In 1968, 1969, 1970, 1971, and 1973, under five different judges, he won the Chow Chow Club National Specialty, a record in Chows for parent club Specialties. His list of champion progeny is impressive, and he is found in the pedigrees of some of our most distinguished winning Chow Chows of the present.

Liontamer High Performance, just starting out on an already successful show career, belongs to Desmond J. Murphy and Stonybrook Kennels.

Liontamer's son, Champion Ah Sid Liontamer Jamboree, co-owned by Dr. Draper and Desmond Murphy, was handled by Mr. Murphy to Number Six Chow Chow in 1973, 1974, and 1975.

Although the Hetheringtons are no longer breeding Chows, Liontamer Kennels continue under the ownership of Dr. Draper and Mr. Murphy at Monroe, New York. They are doing a bit of breeding although now that both are busy with their judging assignments and Dr. Draper's schedule as a professor is such a full one, only a very occasional litter is planned, and Dr. Draper is not exhibiting any dogs at present.

Desmond Murphy co-owns Champion Don-Lee Chowtime with Susie Donnelly from California and did some outstanding winning with this lovely dog in the late 1970's. Now he co-owns and is showing the Best in Show dog, Champion Jen-Sens China Bear of Palm, with Mae Palm and Sunnybrook Kennels, this dog a most worthy descendant of the original Liontamer.

Rising above adversity, a soaking wet Ch. Jen-Sen's China Bear of Palm brings home another Group First for co-owners Desmond J. Murphy, Mike Larizzo and Mae Palm.

Ch. Eastward Liontamer of Elstar, a truly *great* Chow Chow, winning the Non-Sporting Group at Tuxedo Park Kennel Club. Ted Young, Jr., handling for Mr. and Mrs. Robert Hetherington and Dr. Samuel Draper. Mrs. Alexander C. Schwartz, Jr., presenting the trophy.

Palm

Earl and Mae Palm purchased their first Chow Chow back in 1945, the year in which their first child was born. This Chow helped them to raise their four sons, guarded the family and farm, loved hunting pheasants, and was sadly missed by the entire family when they finally lost her at fifteen years of age.

Of course they had to have another Chow, so Palm Miss Chubby from Beulah Chapman's Kennels joined the family. Winifred Kasten of "Fu King" saw her and advised the Palms to register and breed her, which they did. Thus the Palm Kennels at Helenville, Wisconsin, whence have come some of our most outstandingly beautiful Chow Chows, were on their way.

Miss Chubby was bred to Winifred Kasten's Ton Tais Kalidim, he of Nor Ton breeding. This was the first Palm litter, in the early 1960's, and most of the present Palm Chow Chows are descended from this

Ch. Palm's Coquette, by Ch. Liontamer Sunrise of Palm ex Ch. Starcrest Fros-tee, bred and owned by Earl and Mae Palm.

Ch. Palm's Personality Kid at two years of age, by Ch. Liontamer Sunrise of Palm from a Sunrise daughter. A lovely example of the linebred Chows being produced at this famous kennel. Earl and Mae Palm, owners.

breeding. The Palms had Chubby's hips X-rayed when she was nine years old, as the result of which she received OFA #13. Champion Palm's Personality is a great-great-granddaughter of Miss Chubby.

In 1974, Liontamer Kennels and Palm Kennels cooperated to produce Champion Liontamer Sunrise of Palm. He became the background stud for Palm Chow Chows, and his loss at three and a half years of age was a sad one, indeed. But before he died, Sunrise gave the Palms Champion Liontamer Jack, the sire of the magnificent Champion Jen Sen's China Bear of Palm, famous Best in Show winner co-owned by Mae Palm and Desmond Murphy.

The Palms have bred about nineteen champions as of July 1983. In addition to Bear keeping the banner high at present is Champion Charkay's Grand Marnier O'Palm, co-bred by Mae Palm and K.L. Porter. This gorgeous son of Champion Charkay's Lord Calvert O'Palm ex Champion Charkay's Creme Chablis O'Palm is winning Groups and Best in Show honors (along with many admirers) for his co-owners Kathy Porter and M. Tuck Schneider, the latter a famed Brazilian fancier of many breeds.

The Palm breeding program is a combination of their original bloodline, through Miss Chubby, with Liontamer and some Starcrest. Mae Palm likes line-breeding and does a lot of inbreeding, too—obviously with superb results! Good temperament and sound, well-balanced structure are the prime goals at this kennel.

Sa-Mi

Sa-Mi Chow Chows, at Cantonment, Florida, are owned by Sarah Parrish who started her kennel back in the late 1960's with an excellent foundation dog and bitch representing finest bloodlines.

The foundation dog was Champion Warlord's Chu-Jen, a son of the great Champion Starcrest Spy of Poppyland ex a bitch with fourteen points, Tsang Po's Autumn Nocturne, C.D. Bred by Shirley Nelson, this magnificent dog is himself the sire of five or more champions, with many grandchildren who have gained the title as well.

The foundation bitch, Champion Tsang Po's Soo-Chy, was sired by Champion Shanglo's Tishi Ming from Champion Tsang Po's Kwai-Chy and was bred by Hal Allen.

Over the past fifteen years or so, Mrs. Parrish has bred a whole series of champions who add up to an imposing total in numbers and in quality.

Ch. Sa-Mi's Repetitious in November 1981, by Ch. Warlord's Chu-Jen. This is one of the winners from Sa-Mi Chows.

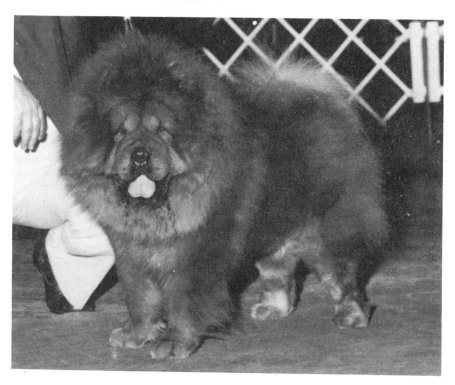

Ch. Sa-Mi's Rustler, "The Duck" to friends, is by Ch. Melody Go That Away Mara ex Ch. Sa-Mi's See My Dolly. Bred, owned and handled by Sarah Parrish, this splendid dog finished his title quickly, at least twice going on to Best of Breed over specials from the classes. As a special he has been defeated only once for Best of Breed.

Sho-Tay

Sho-Tay Chows at Herscher, Illinois, were founded in 1974 by Jill Ullman. The first to finish here was a lovely bitch purchased in January 1976, Champion Sho-Tay's Pekin of Wah-Hu.

Pekin finished at only eleven months old, having begun her career at a match show as a three-month-old puppy, going Best in Match, all-breeds. Although she was only Specialed a few times, she has several Bests of Opposite Sex and one Best of Breed to her credit. She was retired early to become a mother.

Ch. Sho-Tay's Pekin of Wah-Hu, by Wah-Hu's Uncle Tom Z ex Ky-Lin's Quintella, born in 1975, bred by Mary Ann and William Chambers and owned by Sho-Tay Chows.

Ch. Czar, by Ch. Wah-Hu's Chutzpah ex Ky-Lin's Black Star, born in 1975, bred by Mary Ann William is owned by Sho-Tay Chows. Pictured taking a 3-point major en route to the title.

The Ullmans' first male champion, Czar, finished shortly after Pekin. These two excellent Chows formed the foundation of the Sho-Tay line, bringing together a combination of Charmar, Ky-Lin, and Wah-Hu strains. In the last several years Sho-Tay has worked with this stock plus a recent addition of Starcrest for, hopefully, even further improvement of Sho-Tay's very fine line.

Jill Ullman is an avid student of the Chow breed, spending many hours on research of Chow history, bloodlines, problems in the breed, and so on. She is dedicated to producing true quality at Sho-Tay, and she is succeeding very well.

Shanghai

Shanghai Chow Chows belong to K. Jane Weiss, who has been a keen admirer of these handsome dogs since the early 1970's and has certainly distinguished herself as a breeder exhibitor of them during that period of time. The kennel is located in eastern Pennsylvania in what is really ideal climate for Chows. The goal Ms. Weiss has set for herself as a breeder is to produce dogs that are square and powerful in build with strong hindquarters, well balanced, correct both front and rear, with cobby bodies and abundant coats. That she is succeeding well in this ambition becomes abundantly clear as one studies the pictures of her dogs that are included in this book!

One of the leading stud dogs at Shanghai is the beautiful Champion Laral's Excalibur by Weiss, son of Champion Pandee's Dunbar ex Champion Pandee's Panzerella. Among his progeny who have finished to date are Champion Shanghai Enie Menie Mighty Mo, Champion Shanghai Cotton Candy, and Champion Shanghai Cinnamin Bunn, all from Ms. Weiss's noted bitch Champion Cedar Creek's Par-

Shanghai Cinnamon Chows take the whole show! *Left to right,* Ch. Shanghai's Memory's of Meme, Best of Breed over two male specials; Ch. Shanghai's Silver Lining, 5-point major Ch. Shanghai's Cinnamin Bunn, 3-point major. All owned and bred by K. Jane Weiss.

Shanghai's Dynomite at thirteen weeks of age. By Cedar Creek's Charlie Brown ex Ch. Shanghai's Hot Stuff Sure Enuf, all three owned by K. Jane Weiss.

Ch. Shanghai's Enie
Menie Mighty Mo
owned by K. Jane
Weiss, Shanghai
Chow Chows.

ty Girl (Jewell's Supermanchu ex Jemaco Meme of Cedar Creek). Also
there is Champion Shanghai's Mastradomus, along with numerous
others, major pointed as we write, who should certainly be finished
when you are reading this book.

Champion Shanghai's Enie Menie Mighty Mo is following in his
sire's footsteps as an outstanding producer, with some exciting show-
prospect puppies standing by. This 87-pound red male finished with
two five-point majors, a three-point major, and one two-pointer to
complete his title quickly and with ease.

Pandee and Cedar Creek are both strongly represented bloodlines in
Ms. Weiss's breeding program, and she has several Cedar Creek
Chows in residence at Shanghai in addition to the aforementioned
Champion Cedar Creek's Party Girl. They include Cedar Creek Miss
Muffet, the dam of Champion Kitts Macho Man, and Cedar Creek's
Charlie Brown, the sire of Champion Shanghai's Dynomite.

Sunswept

Sunswept Chow Chow Kennels, owned by Barbara A. Durst, are located on 50 beautiful acres at Parkton, Maryland, where Barbara and her husband, Glenn Durst, reside. The kennels number some 40 adult Chows. Twenty-six of them are champions, of which eighteen are home bred, these figures as of July 1983.

Barbara grew up with a Chow, but when he died he was not replaced, simply because in those days despite many efforts to locate another Chow, one could not be found.

Am. and Can. Ch. Sunswept Tonka for four consecutive years has placed on the Top Ten list for Chow Chows in the United States. Bred and owned by Barbara Durst.

Littermates taking Best of Breed and Best of Opposite Sex at Danville Kennel Club, 1977, judged Mrs. Heywood Hartley. Ch. Sunswept The Apache *(left)* and Ch. Sunswept San Yemassee are by Ch. Tonto of Wu San ex Ch. Masterpiece Chatelaine. Bred and owned by Barbara Durst.

Several years of Mrs. Durst's life went into the raising of her four children, but always the family was surrounded by many animals. Mrs. Durst has owned a Dalmatian, an English Springer Spaniel, and a Chesapeake Bay Retriever, and for a goodly period of time she bred and showed Miniature Poodles. Along with the dogs there were horses, a pet raccoon (now eleven years old), two darling monkeys, birds, fish, and several cats, as Barbara Durst says "just thrown in for good measure."

It has always been Barbara Durst's dream to produce an all-champion breeding kennel. With the Chow deep in her heart, she set out to attain that goal! The foundation bitch for Sunswept Chows was obtained in 1972. This was a red named Masterpiece Chatelaine which Barbara showed to her championship. She was a mixture of new and old bloodlines, going back to Ky-Lin. A year later the foundation black stud dog Champion Tonto of Wu San was added. He was eight

Ch. Sunswept Elegant Entry, red bitch born September 1982, by Am. and Can. Ch. Sunswept Tonka ex Sunswept Keeka, handled by Susan Cline for breeder-owner Mrs. Barbara Durst.

years old at the time, carrying an old bloodline back to Champion Loy Jean's Chi Yan Kid and Champion Ghat de la Moulaine. There was a method behind Mrs. Durst's madness. Knowing that there were great dogs in those old bloodlines, she wanted to bring the fine qualities forward. With the union of this dog and this bitch, Sunswept began. Both also became top producers. And Barbara Durst is well pleased with the fact that in eight years she produced eighteen champions, all going back to the original dog and bitch.

Mrs. Durst describes herself as a slow and careful breeder whose choice for breeding is only the best possible quality. She also does not believe in overproduction, flooding the market with superfluous Chows to be mistreated, misused, or mishandled. When she sells a Chow, she does not choose a Chow for the people. She chooses the people for the Chow.

Temperament and soundness are the two most important factors in the breeding program at Sunswept. Mrs. Durst is concerned over the fact that many breeders are concentrating mainly on overdone heads, despite the fact that they are often accompanied by breathing problems, no length of neck, bodies too long, and legs too short, making for

Ch. Sunswept Saucity (Ch. Sunswept Mr. Zephyr ex Ch. Masterpiece Chatelaine) finished her title as a puppy, handled by Susan Cline for Barbara Durst.

Ch. Sunswept Tequesta, by Ch. Tonto of Wu San ex Ky-Lin's Sun Glo, bred and owned by Barbara F. Durst.

lack of balance. To her there is nothing more beautiful than a well-balanced Chow in motion. In her own breeding program, Mrs. Durst likes a moderate head, temperament, and soundness, which gives one a truly functional Chow Chow.

No one more thoroughly enjoys dog shows than does Barbara Durst. However, her full schedule prevents her from getting to them nearly as often as she would like. And besides, as she says, "I must stay home and design the product." Thus Sunswept Chows are handled by Susan Cline, who Mrs. Durst comments is "a truly dedicated handler who devotes her time and love to my dogs."

The most famous of the Sunswept Chows to date is, of course, the magnificent American and Canadian Champion Sunswept Tonka, who is a son of these original two Chows at Sunswept, Champion Tonto of Wu San and Champion Masterpiece Chatelaine. A home-bred, Tonka started his career at six months of age by taking Best of Breed over several Specials at Upper Marlboro Kennel Club under judge Bryon Munson, then on to a Group second under judge Vincent Perry. Now he is retired with well over 250 Bests of Breed, many Groups, and other important honors which kept him on the Top Ten lists for four consecutive years, the only Chow to Mrs. Durst's knowledge who has held a position on the Top Ten four consecutive times.

Tonka has made an impressive mark on the breed as a stud dog as well as in the ring. It seems certain that we will be seeing descendants of this great dog standing in the winners circle for many years to come.

Taichung

Taichung Chow Chows at Olympia, Washington, are owned by Laura Perkinson, formerly a Collie breeder who since the early 1970's has been involved with Chows.

Among Ms. Perkinson's favorites are an exciting puppy, Taichung Justin of Mike Mar, bred by and purchased from Michael Wolf of Mike Mar fame. This youngster, at seven months, already has five points toward his title and is a son of Champion Kobys Cassanova of Sweetkins.

Then there is Taichung Dark Design, with ten points toward championship in July 1983, a combination of Plainacres and Prophet breeding, and Taichung Samantha, with ten points, a homebred combining Plainacres-Liontamer-Jamaco lines.

By the time you are reading this book, all three of these lovely Chows should be champions.

Ch. Lorraine's Skarlet of Samchow is one of the handsome Chow Chows belonging to Meribeth Correll at Wu Li Chow Chows.

The Wu Li Impressario (Can. and Am. Ch. Mi Tu's Han Su Shang ex Bu Dynasty's The Empress) bred and owned by Meribeth Correll.

Wu Li

Wu Li Chow Chows came into being when, during 1979, Meribeth Correll and Keith Propp of Lawrence, Kansas, began to consider owning and showing a quality member of this breed. The Northern dogs were their favorites, and the Chow Chow personality very quickly had won their hearts. Champion Lorraine's Skarlet of Samchow soon came to live in their home. Skarlet earned her A.K.C. championship by the time she was one year of age, and was followed by Lorraine's Cagni of Samchow who gained his title the same year, also at one year's age. Both Champion Skarlet and Champion Cagni were the dark mahogany color so cherished by Chow Chow fanciers.

With the goal of producing an even finer Chow Chow, Champion Skarlet was bred to Bu Dynasty's Heavy Duty, owned by Herb and Joan Williams and Fred Peddie of Toronto, Canada. The lovely litter which resulted included The Wu Li Ballerina, The Wu Li Maestra, and Wu Li's Peking Prince, C.D., owned by Jim and Debbie Keen. At this time Meribeth and Keith chose Wu Li as their kennel name.

Eventually Wu Li became the home of Bu Dynasty's The Empress, daughter of the multiple Best in Show winning Canadian and American Champion Bu Dynasty's Shang Hi, granddaughter of the Canadian and American Champion Mi Tu's Han Su Shang of Bu Dynasty. The Empress produced The Wu Li Virtuoso and The Wu Li Impressario, young dogs for whom the future should be bright.

Although it is a very young kennel, Wu Li has a standard of excellence which it is keeping high, priding itself on good temperament and quality. Today and in years to come Meribeth and her daughter, Dawn Correll, plan to continue breeding and showing outstanding Wu Li Chow Chows.

The Wu Li Ballerina, a homebred daughter of Bu Dynasty's Heavy Duty ex Ch. Lorraine's Skarlett of Samchow, belonging to Meribeth Correll.

Bu Dynasty's The Empress, by Can. and Am. Ch. Bu Dynasty's Shang Hi ex Ralbenic Petticoat Lane was bred by Joan and Herb Williams and Fred Peddie of the famous Canadian kennel, Bu Dynasty, and is owned by Meribeth Correll.

This is Mi-Pao's Schatzi, born December 1979, by Ch. Cesar Kwei Jang (Holland) ex Can. Ch. Mi Pao's Bena, bred by F.P.A. Odenkirchen, Waterdown, Ontario. Owned by Mr. and Mrs. Maurice Lacroix, Bromont, Quebec.

Chapter 5

Chow Chows in Canada

Chow Chow popularity in Canada has been impressive over the years, and the success with which dogs from there have met, both at home and abroad, has been very noteworthy.

British Columbia
Among Chow breeders in western Canada, Mrs. Madge P. Wiesman at Vancouver, British Columbia, has had some outstanding dogs since the establishment of her Foo H'Sing Kennels back in 1957.

Another highly successful Chow Chow breeder from the British Columbia area is James Campbell, owner of the Cambellyn Kennels, which has produced many an outstanding winner. Mr. Campbell owned American, Canadian, and Bermudian Champion Starcrest Surmount, a famous winner whom he handled to numerous exciting victories, including Best Non-Sporting Dog at the invitational "show of shows," Canada's most prestigious event, under Canadian Kennel Club President Mrs. Hilda Pugh. This great dog died in 1982 at twelve years of age, leaving a legacy of fine descendants to carry on his quality.

Mr. Campbell not long ago decreased the number of dogs in his kennel, at which time he sold the exciting American, Canadian, and Bermudian Champion Jen-Jen O'Cambellyn to Phyllis Castleton of Anchorage, Alaska. Jen-Jen is busily putting Chow Chows on the map in Alaska, and during the three years since Ms. Castleton acquired him, he has only once been out of the Group awards.

Ontario
The Ontario region might well be called a hotbed of Chow Chow activity, as a number of noted breeders are located there.

Of course Bu Dynasty Kennels, belonging to Joan and Herb Williams and J.C.F. Peddie, are known throughout the Chow Chow world owing to the importance of their great dog, Canadian and American Champion Mi-Tu's Han Su Shang, bred by Pat Robb in Canada, sired by the Williams-Peddie owned Specialty and Best in Show winner, Canadian and American Champion Foo H'Sing's Mr. Linn Wu. Shang was Best of Breed at Westminster in 1974 from the classes, from where he went on to an imposing career filled with honors in both the United States and Canada. His wins in the United States, in addition to Groups and Bests in Show, include Best of Breed at the National Specialty. While in Canada he was the Top Show Dog All-Breeds for at least one year, among literally hundreds of exciting wins and honors—super dog in every sense of the word!

Numerous other Chows, owned or raised at Bu Dynasty, have scored brilliant careers in Canada and in the United States. The kennel was founded in 1963.

F.P.A. Odenkirchen, Waterdown, Ontario, founded his Mi-Pao Kennels during the 1950's, and his lovely dogs are behind many a famous kennel and winner in various sections of Canada. The breeding program here goes back into European bloodlines as much of the foundation stock featured both Dutch and Belgian dogs, and, indirectly, those from English kennels. Stud dogs of special influence here have been the Belgian import, International Champion Chang-Shi Hong-Kwong, and Hi-Bo's Adiraja.

Mi-Tu Chows were founded by R.D. Robb at Aurora, Ontario, in 1965 when a bitch was purchased from Mi-Pao Kennels, and they have produced some excellent winning Chows, known in both the States and Canada.

Mrs. Yan Paul, now living in Florida and still a popular dog show judge as she has been over the years, operated the Suyan Kennels, established in the early 1930's, where for many years she raised Chows of quality who became famed winners.

Mrs. Hanna K. Kuester made her Hanchow Kennels, located at Kingston, Ontario, well known. She started breeding Chows (after owning the breed since 1943) during the early 1950's.

Chi-Kwang Kennels, owned by Mrs. M.J. Nattrass, at Pickering, Ontario, bred the first Chow Chow in Canada ever to gain the Best Puppy in Show award. Mrs. Barbara Kristoff, of Toronto, started Champad Kennels in the late 1960's and has owned such dogs as American and Canadian Champions Starcrest Peek-A-Boo of Ho Sen and the noted Starcrest Surmount (who eventually went to James Campbell in British Columbia).

Am., Can., and Bda. Ch. Starcrest Surmount, owner-handled by James Campbell, Surrey, B.C., Canada, was a noted winner and the sire of Phyllis Castleton's famed Am., Can., Bda. Ch. Jen Jen O'Cambellyn.

Can. Ch. Bo-Bleu of Chenango, by Pappy Foo Manchu ex Ming Chow La Moulaine, bred by Ronald and Kathleen Ely of California, winning a Non-Sporting Group placement under the author at St. Francis 1983. Owned and handled by Mrs. Lucille Joly, Pincourt, Quebec.

It was not until 1973 when Keba-Yan Kennels started to become active in Chows, under the ownership of Mrs. Patricia Young and her husband in Ontario.

Sinkiang Kennels had their beginning in 1966, when Mrs. N.V. McEachern started out with Chow Chows. Her dogs have included many champions of type and quality who have won well for her in keen competition.

Nancy Meisner, Utopia, Ontario, has been showing a very handsome young dog, a homebred by Ch. Mi-Pao's Black Knight ex Mi-Pao's Echowood, which we have seen when judging in Canada. He is Lioning Mandarin, and he will undoubtedly be a champion by the time you are reading this.

Quebec

On a recent judging assignment in Quebec, just at the time when I was gathering material for this book, I was very favorably impressed by the excellent quality of the Chow Chows exhibited under me and by the enthusiasm and dedication of the Chow breeders in this area with whom I later talked and discussed the breed. I asked each for pictures of their dogs and a description of their kennels and their activities, determined to do a special part of this chapter dedicated to the Chows and their owners and breeders from Quebec.

Lucille Joly, of Pincourt, whose kennel identification is "Lu," is one of the newer breeders, her first Chow Chow litter having been born in December 1982 and consisting of five beautiful show-type puppies from Celebrity Annabelle, her red foundation female, from Don-Lee bloodlines. A female from this litter will be used in breeding.

Canadian Champion Bo-Bleu of Chanango, by Pappy Foo Manchu ex Ming Chow La Moulaine, was bred by Kathleen Ely of California and now belongs to Mrs. Joly. This is a gorgeous dog in type, soundness, and quality who finished his title quite handily, is two and a half years of age, and should prove a valuable producer as a sire. A newly finished champion, this quality blue dog is an asset to any kennel.

Mr. and Mrs. Maurice Lacroix, of Bromont, are owners of the excellent black male, Canadian Champion Minsh Chi Go, sired by Champion Lishimin Chance By Minsh ex Champion Mi-Pao's Akas; he was born in November 1980 and was bred by Mrs. Armin Krupp. Chi Go has done some good winning for Mr. and Mrs. Lacroix and is also proving his worth as a sire.

The red female, Mi-Pao's Schatzi, born in December 1979, has interesting breeding behind her, being by Champion Cesar Kwei-Jang, a dog from Holland, ex Champion Mi-Pao's Bena. Her breeder is F.P.A. Oderkirchen from Waterdown, Ontario. She is on the way to her championship in Canada.

Then there is the lovely cream male, Golden Nugget, born August 1979, bred by Hermann P. Spies of Westmount, P.Q., who carries top American bloodlines in his pedigree including Starcrest, Ky-Lin, Pandee, Nor-Ton, and Shang Tai. There is also a cream female of these same bloodlines, Ginger, doing well for Mr. and Mrs. Lacroix.

Misty de Guiberdy, bred by Guy Bertrand, Granby, P.Q., is a five-year-old red female. And there is another very nice red female, Lacroix's Trudy, from Misty sired by Golden Nugget, at the Lacroix Kennel.

Mr. and Mrs. Lacroix and their young sons are great admirers of the

Can. Ch. Minsh Spike (Hanchow Fortune Cookie ex Can. Ch. Minsh Peppie) with owner Mrs. Armin Krupp, St. Eustache, Quebec.

Chow Chow, thoroughly enjoying their association with the breed.

Gerry and Marge Ste. Marie are at Brossard, Quebec, and had been breeding and showing Saint Bernards for a number of years when Mrs. Ste. Marie suddenly started to feel left out as her husband, in his enthusiasm, kept taking over their big dogs. Finally she decided that she would find a dog of her own whom she could handle herself and certainly "without his well-intended interference." Thus the first of the Chows was acquired.

Mr. and Mrs. Ste. Marie have been breeding Chows now since the early 1970's. Actually most of their Chows have come from well-established and respected American kennels such as Audrich, Tea-

Can. Ch. Minsh Chico is one of the handsome Chows owned by Mr. and Mrs. Maurice Lacroix, Bromont, Quebec.

Can. and Bda. Ch. Audrich Dooley O'Toole, by Plainacres Charman Fella ex Gorschall's Chada. Bred by Audrey E. Meaney and Richard M. Meaney. Owned by Marge Ste. Marie, Brossard, Quebec.

Can. Ch. Von Casumar's Black Night, by Von Casumar's Just-In-Thyme ex Plainacres Wun Nite Dream. Owner-bred by Marge Ste. Marie, Brossard, Quebec.

bear, Plainacres, Starcrest, and Chinabear. Thus they have the leading bloodlines behind them. Canadian and Bermudian Champion Audrich Dooley O'Toole did a fair amount of winning for them in the ring, taking many Group placements both in Canada and in Bermuda.

Canadian Champion Chinabear Waggin' Master finished his title very early in his show career and is still shown occasionally. Canadian Champion Von Casumar's Black Night, bred by the Ste. Maries, has taken many breed wins in his time and now sits back to allow his sister and her progeny to do their thing.

Some of the most handsome Chow Chows I have seen in the Quebec area have been those bearing the Minsh kennel identification, owned by Mr. and Mrs. Armin Krupp of St. Eustache. The Krupps were in the Canadian Air Force and were once stationed in the Black Forest area of Germany, near Baden-Baden. While attending a picnic at their base, "out bounced this baby Chow." He was just three months old, and, as Mrs. Krupp says, "I did not even know what breed he was then, but I knew I had to have one." He was like a little teddy bear, and the two Krupp sons, at the time aged three and four years old, fell in love as promptly as did their mother with this adorable dog.

The Krupps looked immediately for the puppy's owners, who told them where this puppy had been purchased. So off they went "to

Can. Ch. Chance by Minsh, black male, at four years of age, by Ch. Starcrest Black Hussar ex Ch. Minsh Chia; and Can. Ch. Mi-Pao's Akas, red female at seven years, by Mi-Pao's Itam ex T' Saigon Joanne. From the Minsh Kennels of Mrs. Armin Krupp, St. Eustache, Quebec.

become owners and slaves to our first Chow Chow." The Krupps selected a female, which they named Hexe (meaning "witch" in German). By the time Hexe had reached a year's age, the Krupps had decided that she should have another Chow as a companion, which led to the purchase of their first male Chow, called Baron. When the Krupps returned to Canada, of course both their Chows accompanied them. Hexe, none the less adored, had turned out to be of pet quality and the Krupps decided that they would enjoy a good one for show and breeding. Consequently they visited Mi-Pao's Kennels, where they purchased Champion Mi-Pao's Akas, known as "Penny." In every way "Penny" was a complete success, turning out to be a wonderful mother, show dog, and pet. Her daughter, Champion Minsh Chia, was bred to Hanna Kuester's Champion Starcrest Black Hussar, and from this came their handsome Champion Minsh Chance. Chance was bred back to his mother "Penny," producing the lovely black girl Champion Minsh Darleen. Then a granddaughter of Champion Don Lee's Prophet was bred to Chance, from which breeding came Minsh Me Buddy. Buddy, who has done well in match shows, will be starting out on his career at about the time we are writing, and to quote Mrs. Krupp, "To us he is everything we ever wanted in our Chows." Plans for the future include a breeding between Buddy and Darleen, from which more exciting youngsters are expected.

The Krupps feel that a Chow is the only breed of dog they will ever own. They are so loving and will guard you with their lives, as Mrs. Krupp points out, and after fourteen years of Chow ownership the Krupps are even more enthusiastic over the breed than they were when they started. The Krupp sons are now in their mid-teens, sharing completely their parents' opinion of these wonderful dogs.

Chows in Quebec are very well owned, indeed, and it was heartwarming to note the enthusiasm and dedication of the breeders whom we had the pleasure of meeting at Bromont.

Opposite page: Can. Ch. Peppie by Minsh at nine months old, by Ch. Chance by Minsh ex Minsh Angel. One of the many fine Chows at Minsh Kennels, Mrs. Armin Krupp, St. Eustache, Quebec, Canada.

Sedna Bhu Dina is one of the lovely Chow Chows owned by Mrs. C.J. Reed, Sedna Chow Chows, Guildford, New South Wales.

Chapter 6

Chow Chows in Australia

Australia has become a very much involved part of our world of purebred dogs during recent years. Many fine kennels are breeding there, importations have been brought from all parts of the world, and the important Royal Shows are huge, filled with quality and keen competition. The enthusiasm of these people is very heartwarming, and we admire the fine quality dogs being produced in their kennels.

An especially interesting story is that of the Sedna Chow Chows, belonging to Mrs. C.J. Reed at Guildford in New South Wales.

Mrs. Reed started to breed Chows about sixteen years ago, which would be around 1968, but her own and her husband's association with the breed goes back 'way beyond that time. The Reeds had Samoyeds before the Chow Chows; Mr. Reed, however, had owned a Chow before he left the service and he never forgot about that dog or stopped talking of the breed. The first Chow owned by Mr. Reed was given to him by a Buddhist monk. These dogs, as we all know, are not *sold* but are sometimes *presented* as a gift. While stationed in Japan and riding in a jeep, the young soldier came upon this monk with a Chow on a lead and offered him a ride. The monk was walking his Chow Chow dog to another monastery to be used at stud. A close association followed between the two men following this incident, with Mr. Reed visiting the monastery frequently and giving the monk a lift whenever he was going any distance.

When the soldier left for Korea, the monk called him in and told him that there was a litter of puppies by this dog, which Mr. Reed had come to much admire, and he said, "There are four pups, and when you leave there must be four left." Going for a final look at them, the soldier quickly noted that actually there were *five* puppies in the litter, one with a big bow tied around his neck. As I am sure you all have

109

In the *foreground*, Sedna The Genesis, with Sedna Bhu Dina *behind*. Both Chows from Sedna Kennels.

guessed by now, this puppy was slated to be a gift for the soldier! He was named Caesar and went to Korea with his new master, but sad to report the dog was killed there when only about eight months old. This dog was never forgotten!

Since purchasing her own first Chow in 1968, Mrs. Reed has never looked back; she notes: "I think Chow Chows will feature in our lives for a long time to come, as I have a four-year-old granddaughter already thoroughly 'Chow minded' through and through. She owns her own Chow and is talking now about Bonnie having babies and about keeping one of them. So you see, once having been bitten they stay in your blood."

The Sedna Chows are a handsome group, indeed. Tsulin Bhuda, who would seem to be headman here, was bred by Liz Simpson of Victoria and has an imported Canadian sire, Bu Dynasty the Revelation. Bhuda's great-grandsire is the famous Champion Mi Tus Han Su Shang, owned by Herb Williams of Canada's noted Bu Dynasty Kennels.

110

Sedna Chihli Te at five months, by Aust. Ch. Zebedee Te Karara ex Aust. Ch. Chuanchow Lui Ling, won the Bitch Challenge at the October 1983 Spring Fair Dog Show. She and her brother, Sedna Yung Te, between them won 17 Baby and Minor Puppy Sweepstakes, 15 Groups, and a Best Baby Puppy in Show. Owned by Mrs. C.J. Reed.

Eight-week-old Chow Chow puppies at Mrs. C.J. Reed's Sedna Kennels.

Aust. Ch. Hoisam Lucky, born January 1978, won Challenge Dog and Best of Breed at the 1981 Sydney Royal Easter Show judged by Mr. Bobby James, U.K. Lucky is owned by D. and C. Messnarz, Hoisam Kennels, Bradbury, New South Wales.

Sedna Chihli Tee and Sedna Yung Te are homebreds winning well. They are descended from Weircroft, Ukwong, Kwaisay, and Stapleton lines, the dogs behind them having been imported to Australia by various fanciers.

At present there are nine Chows at Sedna, the oldest being fourteen years of age.

Hoisam Chow Chows are located at Bradbury in New South Wales and belong to D. and C. Messnarz. The kennel name was coined from a combination of the names of the first two Chows here, in the early 1970's, who started these fanciers' wonderful love for the breed.

In 1978 Mr. and Mrs. Messnarz had a litter of eight puppies born to their handsome bitch. So involved did they become with these attractive babies that they ended up keeping four of them, two of whom turned out to be very special and have brought exciting wins and true pleasure to their breeder-owners. These are Australian Champion Hoisam Fuji and Australian Champion Hoisam Lucky.

112

Fuji in 1980 won Challenge Bitch and Runner Up Best in Show at the Chow Chow Club Specialty, judged by Mrs. Sheila Wakeman from the United Kingdom. The following year she was Challenge Bitch at the great Sydney Royal Easter Show under Mr. Bobby James (U.K.) and in 1982 was Reserve Challenge Bitch at this event under judge Mrs. James E. Clark from the United States.

During 1983 this excellent bitch won Best in Show at the Chow Chow Specialty, judged by Mr. John Rowles from New South Wales, and Challenge Bitch at the Sydney Royal Easter Show (Mr. Gadston, judge, U.K.). For the future many further good wins would seem likely.

The 1981 Easter Show was particularly thrilling for Hoisam Chow Chows, as there Champion Hoisam Lucky took the Dog Challenge, then Best of Breed over his sister Fuji, making it truly a "clean sweep" for these enthusiastic breeders.

The well-known winner, Aust. Ch. Hoisam Fuji, a homebred belonging to D. and C. Messnarz.

True magnificence in a Chow Chow head! Ch. Don-Lee Chowtime, co-owned by Susie Donnelly of California and Desmond J. Murphy of Monroe, New York.

Chapter 7

Standards of the Breed

The standard of the breed, to which one hears such frequent reference whenever purebred dogs are the subject of discussion, is the word picture of the ideal specimen of that breed of dog. This standard outlines, in specific detail, each and every feature of the specific breed, both in physical characteristics and in temperament, minutely describing the dog literally "from whisker to tail," creating for the reader a complete mental picture of what is to be considered correct and what is not; the features comprising "breed type"; and the probable temperament and behavior patterns of typical members of the breed.

The standard is the guide for breeders endeavoring to produce quality dogs and for fanciers wishing to learn what is considered beautiful in these dogs; and it is the tool with which judges work in evaluating and reaching their decisions in the show ring. The dog it describes as ideal is the one which we seek as we look at and compare individuals.

Prior to the adoption of a breed standard, or any revisions to same, endless hours have been spent by dedicated fanciers selected from among the most knowledgeable and respected members of the parent club for the task of studying the background of the breed, searching out the earliest histories and breed descriptions from the country of origin and along the way throughout the breed's development. This committee's recommendations then come before the entire membership of the parent Specialty Club for further study and discussion, and then they are presented to the American Kennel Club from which approval must be granted prior to the standard or its revisions becoming effective.

From earliest times, most breeds have had as their standards, usually informally written descriptions of what owners of the dogs have considered important in developing dogs to fulfill their working requirements and the purposes for which these early dogs were intended. As

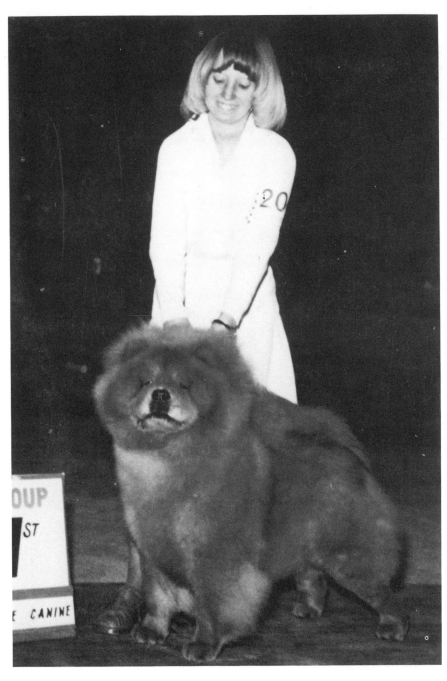

Am., Can., Bda. Ch. Jen-Jen O'Cambellyn handled by Kim Campbell to one of his numerous first in Group awards. Phyllis Castleton, owner, Anchorage, Alaska.

116

This seven-month-old puppy placing in Non-Sporting Group is now Ch. Koby Sweetkins Body Builder (Ch. Tsang Po's Storm Trooper ex Plainacres Wen Su of Koby), bred by Steve and Wendy Kobrzyck, owned by Art Friedman and Michael Wolf, handled here by Bobby Barlow.

117

time progressed, more emphasis has been placed on appearance of the dogs and their beauty. Even so, it should never be forgotten that the majority of breeds were originally developed to assist man in some specific manner and that this basic factor should remain ever present in our effort to preserve those qualities which were involved with the original creation of the breed.

American Standard

The following standard was approved by the American Kennel Club in March 1941.

GENERAL APPEARANCE: A massive, cobby, powerful dog, active and alert, with strong, muscular development and perfect balance. Body squares with height of leg at shoulder; head, broad and flat, with short, broad, and deep muzzle, accentuated by a ruff; the whole supported by straight, strong legs. Clothed in a shining, offstanding coat, the Chow is a masterpiece of beauty, dignity, and untouched naturalness.

HEAD: Large and massive in proportion to size of dog, with broad, flat skull; well filled under the eyes; moderate stop; and proudly carried. *Expression*—Essentially dignified, lordly, scowling, discerning, sober, and snobbish—one of independence. *Muzzle*—Short in comparison to length of skull; broad from eyes to end of nose, and of equal depth. The lips somewhat full and overhanging. *Teeth*—Strong and level, with a scissors bite; should neither be overshot, nor undershot. *Nose*—Large, broad, and black in color. (Disqualification—nose spotted or distinctly other color than black, *except* in blue Chows, which may have solid blue or slate noses.) *Tongue*—A blue-black. The tissues of the mouth should approximate black. (Disqualification—tongue red, pink, or obviously spotted with red or pink). *Eyes*—Dark, deep-set, of moderate size, and almond shaped. *Ears*—Small, slightly rounded at tip, stiffly carried. They should be placed wide apart, on top of the skull, and set with a slight, forward tilt. (Disqualification—drop ear or ears. A drop ear is one which is not stiffly carried or stiffly erect, but which breaks over at any point from its base to its tip.)

BODY: Short, compact, with well-sprung ribs, and let down in the flank.

NECK: Strong, full, set well on the shoulders.

SHOULDERS: Muscular, slightly sloping.

CHEST: Broad, deep, and muscular. A narrow chest is a serious fault.

BACK: Short, straight, and strong.

LOINS: Broad, deep, and powerful.

TAIL: Set well up and carried closely to the back, following line of spine at start.

FORELEGS: Perfectly straight, with heavy bone and upright pasterns.

HIND LEGS: Straight-hocked, muscular, and heavy boned. *Feet*— Compact, round, catlike, with thick pads.

GAIT: Completely individual. Short and stilted because of straight hocks.

COAT: Abundant, dense, straight, and off-standing; rather coarse in texture with a soft, woolly undercoat. It may be any clear color, solid throughout, with lighter shadings on ruff, tail, and breechings.

DISQUALIFICATIONS: Nose spotted or distinctly other color than black, except in blue Chows, which may have solid blue or slate noses. Tongue red, pink or obviously spotted with red or pink. Drop ear or ears.

British and Australian Standard

The British standard for the Chow Chow is the same as the Australian standard for the breed.

CHARACTERISTICS: A well-balanced dog, leonine in appearance, with proud dignified bearing; loyal yet aloof; unique in its stilted gait and bluish-black tongue.

GENERAL APPEARANCE: An active, compact, short-coupled and well balanced dog, well knit in frame, with tail carried well over the back.

HEAD AND SKULL: Skull flat and broad, with little stop, well filled out under the eyes. Muzzle moderate in length, broad from the eyes to the point (not pointed at the end like a fox). Nose black, large and wide in all cases (with the exception of cream and white in which case a light-coloured nose is permissible and in blues and fawns a self-coloured nose); but in all colours a black nose is preferable.

EYES: Dark and small, preferably almond-shaped (in blue or fawn dog a light colour is permissible).

EARS: Small, thick, slightly rounded at the tip, carried stiffly erect but placed well forward over the eyes and wide apart, which gives the dog the peculiar characteristic expression of the breed, viz., a scowl.

MOUTH: Teeth strong and level, giving scissor bite. Tongue

bluish black. Flews and roof of mouth black. Gums preferably black.
NECK: Strong, full, set well on the shoulders and slightly arched.
FOREQUARTERS: Shoulders muscular and sloping. Forelegs perfectly straight, of moderate length and with good bone.
BODY: Chest broad and deep. Back short, straight and strong. Loins powerful.
HINDQUARTERS: Hindlegs muscular and hocks well let down and perfectly straight which are essential in order to produce the Chow's characteristic stilted gait.
FEET: Small, round and catlike, standing well on the toes.
TAIL: Set high and carried well over the back.
COAT: Abundant, dense, straight and stand-off. Outer coat rather coarse in texture and with a soft woolly undercoat. The Chow Chow is a profusely coated dog and balance should therefore be assessed when the coat is at its natural length.
COLOUR: Whole coloured black, red, blue, fawn, cream or white, frequently shaded but not in patches or parti-coloured (the underpart of tail and back of thighs frequently of a light colour).
WEIGHT AND SIZE: Minimum height for Chows to be 18 inches, but in every case balance should be the outstanding feature and height left to the discretion of the judges.
FAULTS: Drop-ears, tongue splashed or patchy, tail not carried over the back, parti-coloured, off black noses except in the colours specified, viz., creams, whites, blues or fawns. Any artificial shortening of the coat which alters the natural outline or expression of the dog should be penalised. (The Standard of the smooth variety is identical with the above except that the coat is smooth.)

Interpretation of the American Chow Chow Standard

There is no greater exercise in futility than studying and learning the *words* of the standard of your breed without at the same time learning to *interpret* those words—to understand what it is that they are saying and to perfect the art of applying them as one looks at or examines actual dogs of that breed. The words are meaningless unless one has the art of visualizing the dog being described by them and understanding what it is that they are saying about the breed.

It takes concentration and serious study in order to train one's eye to recognize the correct, to differentiate between the correct and the incorrect, and to evaluate the total dog based on the various components of which he consists. One must develop a mental picture of what the standard means, not just of empty words. One must be able to recognize a correct head; to see the association between high placed hocks and only slightly sloping shoulders with the short, stilted action characteristic of a Chow Chow; to measure by eye the "squareness" demanded by the standard, which is the relationship between length of back and height at the shoulders; to note the rib spring essential to correct body shape and breadth of chest; and so on, through every feature of the total dog. There is a reason for every feature being as it is, which must be realized and understood by the student of the breed prior to full development of one's capacity to evaluate these dogs and to compare one with another. It is a fascinating pursuit which should never be taken lightly, for until the time when you are completely at ease with and fully understand what the standard is putting into words, you simply will not have the ability to make knowledgeable selections as a breeder or as a judge, thus advancing the quality of your kennel or the dogs you show.

Chow Chow fanciers are fortunate in that theirs is a brief, concise, and explicitly stated standard. It says what it means without fanfare and covers quite well the characteristics important to recognize in the breed. Quite possibly this is why it has remained unchanged over so long a period of time, for it is quite true and has frequently been proven that when one starts to re-phrase and elaborate on a standard, that standard easily can become excessively "wordy," creating confusion rather than the desired clarification. In the case of the standard for Chow Chows, everything is right there, presented in an easily understood manner.

As a judge of Chow Chows, to me one of the most distressing tendencies I have noted is lack of balance, not nearly so great a problem several decades back as it is now when so much emphasis has been placed on head and coat, losing sight of the fact that the dog must be *built* like a Chow if he is to look like one and function properly.

The standard states plainly that a Chow Chow is "A massive, cobby, powerful dog." It is difficult for me to understand why these words are so frequently overlooked, especially where cobbiness is concerned, and why judges accept and honor with awards dogs so long of body

Kamara Superbia taking Group Second at a Wampanoag K.C. Match Show. Judge
Cynthia Fonteneau. Owned by Carl and Marcia Boudreau, Kamara Kennels.

and short of leg as to be highly atypical and grotesque in appearance. "Cobbiness" is defined by the American Kennel Club as "short bodied and compact," and this is emphasized by the further description in the Chow Chow's standard of the fact that correctly "the body squares with height of leg at shoulder." What could be more explicit? What could leave less room for misinterpretation?

In looking at a Chow Chow, the features which should first impress you are his balance; his wide, massive head with flat topskull and comparatively short, broad, square muzzle enhanced by slightly rounded, small, stiffly carried and erect ears; his characteristic scowling expression depicting great dignity and brought about by the wrinkles of his forehead; his breadth of chest with strong, straight, heavily boned forelegs; his characteristic stilt-like hind legs which are without noticeable angulation due to only slight bend at the stifle and straightness of hock; and his abundant, offstanding coat featuring a profuse mane framing the head.

On examination, one should find the Chow's nose leather black except in the blues where self color (blue) is acceptable. The tongue must be blue-black, as should the tissues of the mouth. Deviation on these features is a disqualification. The deep-set, almond-shaped dark eyes are important for their part in correct expression.

The manner in which a Chow Chow moves is one of his most individualistic features, and it is also one of the most frequently misunderstood. The conformation of his practically un-angulated hindlegs combined with the only slightly sloping (angulated) shoulders naturally limits his reach and the length of his steps. Thus the Chow moves with quick, short steps. These, however, should be brisk and firm, carrying the dog right along with no sidewinding or wobbling at the joints. The latter fault is a serious one as it is usually caused by a slipping kneecap which is a bad weakness. A correctly moving Chow has plenty of endurance and does not tire easily.

The Chow Chow carries his tail over his back, set high at the root, running along the spine until nearing the tip.

The Chow Chow standard makes no specific demands regarding size of weight beyond that the dog should be well balanced and that height at the shoulders should square with the length of body. Chow experts agree, however, that an average size Chow dog should be from 17 to 20 inches tall and weigh between 55 and 70 pounds, while a bitch should be 16 to 18 inches tall and weigh between 45 to 55 pounds. Remember, though, that these are *not* official limitations, and they do not appear in the standard. We mention them here mainly to give any novices among our readers a general idea of probable Chow size.

Breed disqualifications under the Chow Chow standard involve only color of the nose, tongue, and mouth tissues already discussed, and the ears. The latter are a tremendously important feature of the breed due to their influence on expression. The key words to their correctness involve "small" and "stiffly carried," which they must be for the enhancement of the ideal head. Chow experts agree that Chow ears practically cannot be too small and are more inclined to go to the other extreme. Correctly set on top of the skull (never hanging off to the sides), they are set with just the slightest forward tilt and very stiffly carried. Drop ear, or drop ears, disqualify; thus, it is important that the term be understood. Such an ear folds over, or is broken down, at some point between the base and tip, which can be ascertained by handling it with your fingers. Owing to the heaviness of mane, especially in some of the biggest coated specimens, and the amount of thick hair surrounding the dog's head, the weight of the hair and its profuseness may lead to an impression that the dog's ears drop, or fold over, when actually this is not the case. So check carefully to be sure before deciding whether you are seeing an actual disqualification or just an extremely heavy mane resting its weight on the ears.

Dogs with disqualifications cannot be shown and should not be used for breeding.

The only requisite regarding color of a Chow Chow is that it be clear and solid throughout, with any lighter shadings only on the ruff, tail, and breeches. The most usually seen Chow colors are any shade of red, solid throughout or with the aforementioned shading, or solid black, which should be a *good* black, not sunburned or rusty in appearance. Other solid colors one is seeing quite frequently now are blue, which is a diluted form of black, and cinnamon or fawn, which are diluted forms of red. All permissible Chow Chow colors should be regarded on an equal basis in evaluating the dog for or in the show ring. All are equally desirable, and preferences among them are a personal matter and have nothing to do with requirements of the standard.

Opposite page: Desmond J. Murphy (handling), Mae Palm and Stonybrook Kennels co-own this famed winner, Ch. Jen-Sens China Bear of Palm, a son of Ch. Palm's Liontamer Jack out of Liontamer Fluffy of Ho-San.

GROUP
FIRST
ROCKLAND COUNTY
KENNEL CLUB
1983
ASHBEY

A handsome portrait of Ch. Don Lee Chowtime, owned by Desmond J. Murphy and Susie Donnelly, taken at Tarrytown, New York, September 10th 1978.

Chapter 8

The Smooth-Coated Chow Chow

Although they are unrecognized in the United States, and are not included in the American Kennel Club standard for the breed, there is a smooth-coated variety of Chow Chow in some parts of the world of which we would like to tell our readers, and we include pictures of these handsome dogs. There is a particularly active group of dedicated people in Holland working to preserve the smooth Chow, and they have what is described as "probably the biggest group in the world, but surely in Europe" consisting of about twenty dogs—noteworthy since smooths so nearly completely died out following the Second World War.

In Holland, it is due to the efforts of Mrs. Christina A. Veldhuis, of the Warnsborn Kennels, that the nucleus of smooth Chow fanciers has been active. Mrs. Veldhuis has done much to promote the variety, and has strong supporters, among the most enthusiastic being H.L. and J. Leunissen-Rooseboom who have sent us the photo which accompanies this chapter. The subjects are two of their smooths.

We are told that the smooth Chow Chow, as the breed came to Europe, is as normal as the rough; and since it is a member of the Chow family, this group of breeders feels it should not be neglected. Regarding the present breeding activities in Holland, the Leunissen-Roosebooms are among the most active and are happy at having been able to obtain Warnsborn Shi-Kari from Mrs. Veldhuis. Kari was bred by Mrs. Veldhuis from her smooth bitch Warnsborn Binna and the dark red rough Pandee's New World Ambassador. Kari had one litter of four smooths and one rough with her uncle, brother of Binna, the smooth dog Warnsboro Mombo. The two daughters from her litters subsequently were bred, one with a blue smooth from France, the other with two different red roughs. The results of the three litters

Smooth Chow Chows from Holland. Warnsboro Shi-Kari (*right*) and Anne van het Bossche (*left*). Bitch and dog owned by H.L. and J. Leunissen-Rooseboom, Gronsveld, Holland.

were six dogs and two bitches of the smooth variety and three dogs and four bitches of the rough. One of the two smooth dogs stayed with the Leunissen-Rooseboooms and was mated with a blue rough daughter of a cream smooth in France, four black smooths being the result.

Since smooths must compete in the ring at European shows with the rough Chow Chows, it is not easy going for them, as we are told that the coats are not the only differences. The roughs there have developed a different type, "a more heavy type" than the smooth. The latter, in general, has kept the original early type which smooth breeders have attempted to consolidate.

The smooth-coated Chow is about to become recognized by the Chow Chow Club and the A.K.C. The necessary changes in the standard are now being made and Smooth Chows are already appearing in the United States, attracting an enthusiastic following.

Opposite page: Ch. Ro Don's Mr. Chips at eight and a half years old. This dog, in two and a half years, won 11 All-Breed Bests in Show, 85 Non-Sporting Group Firsts, and 175 Group placements. Owned by Ron Ewing, Kansas City, Kansas, handled by Ken Rensink.

Kamara Superbia at two years taking Best of Breed at Windham County in 1979. Owned by C. and M. Boudreau, Kamara Chow Chows, Rockland, Massachusetts.

Chapter 9

The Purchase of Your Dog or Puppy

Careful consideration should be given to what breed of dog you wish to own prior to your purchase of one. If several breeds are attractive to you, and you are undecided which you prefer, learn all you can about the characteristics of each before making your decision. As you do so, you are thus preparing yourself to make an intelligent choice; and this is very important when buying a dog who will be, with reasonable luck, a member of your household for at least a dozen years or more. Obviously since you are reading this book, you have decided on the breed—so now all that remains is to make a good choice.

It is never wise to just rush out and buy the first cute puppy who catches your eye. Whether you wish a dog to show, one with whom to compete in obedience, or one as a family dog purely for his (or her) companionship, the more time and thought you invest as you plan the purchase, the more likely you are to meet with complete satisfaction. The background and early care behind your pet will reflect in the dog's future health and temperament. Even if you are planning the purchase purely as a pet, with no thoughts of showing or breeding in the dog's or puppy's future, it is essential that if the dog is to enjoy a trouble-free future you assure yourself of a healthy, properly raised puppy or adult from sturdy, well-bred stock.

Throughout the pages of this book you will find the names and locations of many well-known and well-established kennels in various areas. Another source of information is the American Kennel Club (51 Madison Avenue, New York, NY 10010) from whom you can obtain a list of recognized breeders in the vicinity of your home. If you plan to have your dog campaigned by a professional handler, by all means let

Left, Warnsborn Shi-Kari, red smooth bitch, by Pandee's New World Ambassador ex Warnsboro Binna, born in 1978, bred by Chr. A. Veldhuis. *Right,* Anne Van Het Bossche Front, smooth dog, by Warnsborn Mombo ex Warnsborn Shi-Kari, born 1979, bred, and both owned, by H.L. and J. Leunissen-Rooseboom, Gronsveld, Holland.

This is the all-time Top sire in Chow Chow history! Ch. Don-Lee Prophet, owned by the noted Californians, Rick and Reba Donnelly.

Ch. Sweetkins Bachelor Boy, by Ch. Cherie's Angel Dust ex Sweetkins China Syndrome, taking Best of Breed, Trenton Kennel Club 1982. Desmond Murphy judge, Mr. Wolf handling. Bred by Art and Barbara Friedman. Owned by Art Friedman and Michael Wolf.

the handler help you locate and select a good dog. Through their numerous clients, handlers have access to a variety of interesting show prospects; and the usual arrangement is that the handler re-sells the dog to you for what his cost has been, with the agreement that the dog be campaigned for you by him throughout the dog's career. I most strongly recommend that prospective purchasers follow these suggestions, as you thus will be better able to locate and select a satisfactory puppy or dog.

Your first step in searching for your puppy is to make appointments at kennels specializing in the chosen breed, where you can visit and inspect the dogs, both those available for sale and the kennel's basic breeding stock. You are looking for an active, sturdy puppy with bright eyes and intelligent expression and who is friendly and alert; avoid puppies who are hyperactive, dull, or listless. The coat should be clean and thick, with no sign of parasites. The premises on which he was raised should look (and smell) clean and be tidy, making it obvious that the puppies and their surroundings are in capable hands. Should the kennels featuring the breed you intend owning be sparse in your area or not have what you consider attractive, do not hesitate to contact others at a distance and purchase from them if they seem better able to supply a puppy or dog who will please you *so long as it is a recognized breeding kennel of that breed.* Shipping dogs is a regular practice nowadays, with comparatively few problems when one considers the number of dogs shipped each year. A reputable, well-known breeder wants the customer to be satisfied; thus he will represent the puppy fairly. Should you not be pleased with the puppy upon arrival, a breeder such as I have described will almost certainly permit its return. A conscientious breeder takes real interest and concern in the welfare of the dogs he or she causes to be brought into the world. Such a breeder also is proud of a reputation for integrity. Thus on two counts, for the sake of the dog's future and the breeder's reputation, to such a person a *satisfied* customer takes precedence over a sale at any cost.

If your puppy is to be a pet or "family dog," I feel the earlier the age at which it joins your household the better. Puppies are weaned and ready to start out on their own, under the care of a sensible new owner, at about six weeks old; and if you take a young one, it is often easier to train it to the routine of your household and your requirements of it than is the case with an older dog which, even though still a puppy technically, may have already started habits you will find difficult to change. The younger puppy is usually less costly, too, as it stands to

Chows are known for being among the most irresistible puppies of any breed of dog. As a splendid example, here is Shanghai's Dynomite at eight weeks owned by K. Jane Weiss, Shanghai Kennels at Pottsville, Pennsylvania.

Two lovely puppies, typical of the Chows raised by Dusten's Chow Chows, Dusten and John Cox, owners, Sharon, Connecticut. These in the photo are two-and-a-half months old.

Michael Dachel winning the Chow Chow Club Specialty for Mary Vaudo and Zola Coogan with Ch. Wah Hu Red Cloud Sugar Daddy in June 1982. Bred by Mary Ann Chambers.

Ch. Koby Cassanova of Sweetkins, bred by Steve and Wendy Kobryzcki, owned by Mrs. Alan Robson and Mr. Michael Wold, and sired by Ch. T'Sang's Storm Trooper ex Ch. Plainacres Wen Su of Kobys. Handled by Bobby Barlow to Best Non-Sporting under judge Bill Bergum at Rock Creek Kennel Club 1982.

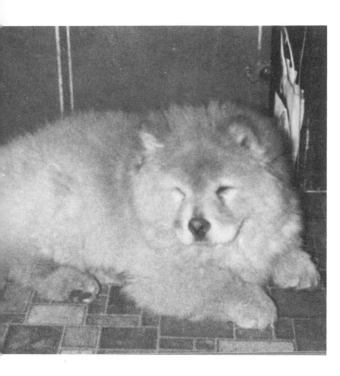

Golden Nugget at 14 weeks of age. Cream male, born August 1979, bred by Hermann P. Spies, Westmount, P.Q. Owned by Mr. and Mrs. Maurice Lacroix, Bromont, P.Q., Canada.

Ch. Lorraine's Skarlet of Sam Chow at six months of age. By Lorraine's Sho Tay Tyger ex Lorraine's Petite Fleur, breeder Lorraine Sanders. Owned by Meribeth Correll, Lawrence, Kansas.

reason the breeder will not have as much expense invested in it. Obviously, a puppy that has been raised to five or six months old represents more in care and cash expenditure on the breeder's part than one sold earlier and therefore should be and generally is priced accordingly.

There is an enormous amount of truth in the statement that "bargain" puppies seldom turn out to be that. A "cheap" puppy, cheaply raised purely for sale and profit, can and often does lead to great heartbreak including problems and veterinarian's bills which can add up to many times the initial cost of a properly reared dog. On the other hand, just because a puppy is expensive does not assure one that is healthy and well reared. I know of numerous cases where unscrupulous dealers have sold for several hundred dollars puppies that were sickly, in poor condition, and such poor specimens that the breed of which they were supposedly members was barely recognizable. So one cannot always judge a puppy by price alone. Common sense must guide a prospective purchaser, plus the selection of a *reliable,* well-recommended dealer whom you know to have well-satisfied customers or, best of all, a specialized breeder. You will probably find the fairest pricing at the kennel of a breeder. Such a person, experienced with the breed in general and with his or her own stock in particular, through extensive association with these dogs has watched enough of them mature to have obviously learned to assess quite accurately each puppy's potential—something impossible where such background is non-existent.

One more word on the subject of pets. Bitches make a fine choice for this purpose as they are usually quieter and more gentle than the males, easier to house train, more affectionate, and less inclined to roam. If you do select a bitch and have no intention of breeding or showing her, by all means have her spayed, for your sake and for hers. The advantages to the owner of a spayed bitch include avoiding the nuisance of "in season" periods which normally occur twice yearly, with the accompanying eager canine swains haunting your premises in an effort to get close to your female, plus the unavoidable messiness and spotting of furniture and rugs at this time, which can be annoying if she is a household companion in the habit of sharing your sofa or bed. As for the spayed bitch, she benefits as she grows older because this simple operation almost entirely eliminates the possibility of breast cancer ever occurring. I personally believe that all bitches should eventually be spayed—even those used for show or breeding when their careers are ended—in order that they may enjoy a happier, healthier old age. Please take note, however, that a bitch who has been

BEST OF BREED

APRIL 17, 1983

Quasi of Kamara at seven and a half months, pictured taking Best of Breed from the puppy classes, now has 18 points in two months of showing. Carl and Marcia Boudreau owners, Rockland, Massachusetts.

Opposite page: A famous Chow Chow from Alaska, Am., Can., Bda. Ch. Jen-Jen O'Cambellyn sired by Am., Can. ex Bda. Ch. Starcrest Surmount, handled by Renee Marcy winning the Group at Kena Kennel Club in August 1982. Owned by Phyllis Castleton of Anchorage.

spayed (or an altered dog) *cannot be shown at American Kennel Club Dog shows once this operation has been performed.* Be certain that you are *not* interested in showing her before taking this step.

Also in selecting a pet, never underestimate the advantages of an older dog, perhaps a retired show dog or a bitch no longer needed for breeding, who may be available quite reasonably priced by a breeder anxious to place such a dog in a loving home. These dogs are settled and can be a delight to own, as they make wonderful companions, especially in a household of adults where raising a puppy can sometimes be a trial.

Everything we have said about careful selection of your pet puppy and its place of purchase applies, but with many further considerations, when you plan to buy a show dog or foundation stock for a future breeding program. Now is the time for an in-depth study of the breed, starting with every word and every illustration in this book and all others you can find written on the subject. The standard of the breed now has become your guide, and you must learn not only the

Appropriately, this Chow puppy is playing in a clump of bamboo in the back garden at Sedna Kennels, Mrs. C.J. Reed, Guildford, New South Wales, Australia.

Ch. Laral's Excalibur by Weiss, by Ch. Pandee's Dunbar ex Ch. Panzee's Panzerella. Breeder, A. Thompson. Owner, K. Jane Weiss, Shanghai Chows.

words but also how to interpret them and how they are applicable in actual dogs before you are ready to make an intelligent selection of a show dog.

If you are thinking in terms of a dog to show, obviously you must have learned about dog shows and must be in the habit of attending them. This is fine, but now your activity in this direction should be increased, with your attending every single dog show within a reasonable distance from your home. Much can be learned about a breed at ringside at these events. Talk with the breeders who are exhibiting. Study the dogs they are showing. Watch the judging with concentration, noting each decision made and attempt to follow the reasoning by which the judge has reached it. Note carefully the attributes of the dogs who win and, for your later use, the manner in which each is presented. Close your ears to the ringside know-it-alls, usually novice owners of only a dog or two and very new to the fancy, who have only derogatory remarks to make about all that is taking place unless they happen to win. This is the type of exhibitor who "comes and goes" through the fancy and whose interest is usually of very short duration owing to lack of knowledge and dissatisfaction caused by the failure to recognize the need to learn. You, as a fancier who we hope will last

143

Ch. Cabaret Joker winning Best in Show under Mrs. Doris Wear at Dayton Kennel Club in 1982, handled by Jamie Richard. Bred and owned by Cabaret Chows, Joan and James Richard, Bay City, Michigan.

DAYTON K.C.

BEST IN SHO

and enjoy our sport over many future years, should develop independent thinking at this stage; you should learn to draw your own conclusions about the merits, or lack of them, seen before you in the ring and thus sharpen your own judgment in preparation for choosing wisely and well.

Note carefully which breeders campaign winning dogs, not just an occasional isolated good one but consistent, homebred winners. It is from one of these people that you should select your own future "star."

If you are located in an area where dog shows take place only occasionally or where there are long travel distances involved, you will need to find another testing ground for your ability to select a worthy show dog. Possibly, there are some representative kennels raising this breed within a reasonable distance. If so, by all means ask permission of the owners to visit the kennels and do so when permission is granted. You may not necessarily buy then and there, as they may not have available what you are seeking that very day, but you will be able to see the type of dog being raised there and to discuss the dogs with the breeder. Every time you do this, you add to your knowledge. Should one of these kennels have dogs which especially appeal to you, perhaps you could reserve a show-prospect puppy from a coming litter. This is frequently done, and it is often worth waiting for a puppy, unless you have seen a dog with which you are truly greatly impressed and which is immediately available.

We have already discussed the purchase of a pet puppy. Obviously this same approach applies in a far greater degree when the purchase involved is a future show dog. The only place at which to purchase a show prospect is from a breeder who raises show-type stock; otherwise, you are almost certainly doomed to disappointment as the puppy matures. Show and breeding kennels obviously cannot keep all of their fine young stock. An active breeder-exhibitor is, therefore, happy to place promising youngsters in the hands of people also interested in showing and winning with them, doing so at a fair price according to the quality and prospects of the dog involved. Here again, if no kennel in your immediate area has what you are seeking, do not hesitate to contact top breeders in other areas and to buy at long distance. Ask for pictures, pedigrees, and a complete description. Heed the breeder's advice and recommendations, after truthfully telling exactly what your expectations are for the dog you purchase. Do you want something with which to win just a few ribbons now and then? Do you want a dog who can complete his championship? Are you thinking of the real

146

A couple of Dusten's kids! Typical of the splendid quality at Dusten and John Cox's kennels, Sharon, Connecticut.

Ch. Ah Sid Liontamer Jamboree owned by Desmond J. Murphy and Dr. Samuel Draper, Liontamer Chow Chows, Monroe, New York.

Opposite page: *(Top)* Ch. Liontamer Sunrise of Palm (Ch. Ah Sid Liontamer Jamboree ex Starcrest Liontamer Memoire) in 1977. Owned by Palm's Chow Chows, Earl and Mae Palm, Helenville, Wisconsin. *(Bottom)* Ch. Sunswept High Roller, born September 1982, by Am. and Can. Ch. Sunswept Tonka ex Ch. Sunswept Keeka. Handled by Susan Cline for breeder-owner Mrs. Barbara Durst, Parkton, Maryland.

"big time" (*i.e.*, seriously campaigning with Best of Breed, Group wins, and possibly even Best in Show as your eventual goal)? Consider it all carefully in advance; then honestly discuss your plans with the breeder. You will be better satisfied with the results if you do this, as the breeder is then in the best position to help you choose the dog who is most likely to come through for you. A breeder selling a show dog is just as anxious as the buyer for the dog to succeed, and the breeder will represent the dog to you with truth and honesty. Also, this type of breeder does not lose interest the moment the sale has been made but when necessary will be right there ready to assist you with beneficial advice and suggestions based on years of experience.

As you make inquiries of at least several kennels, keep in mind that show-prospect puppies are less expensive than mature show dogs, the latter often costing close to four figures, and sometimes more. The reason for this is that, with a puppy, there is always an element of chance, the possibility of its developing unexpected faults as it matures or failing to develop the excellence and quality that earlier had seemed probable. There definitely is a risk factor in buying a show-prospect puppy. Sometimes all goes well, but occasionally the swan becomes an ugly duckling. Reflect on this as you consider available puppies and young adults. It just might be a good idea to go with a more mature, though more costly, dog if one you like is available.

When you buy a mature show dog, "what you see is what you get"; and it is not likely to change beyond coat and condition which are dependent on your care. Also advantageous for a novice owner is the fact that a mature dog of show quality almost certainly will have received show ring training and probably match show experience, which will make your earliest handling ventures far easier.

Frequently it is possible to purchase a beautiful dog who has completed championship but who, owing to similarity in bloodlines, is not needed for the breeder's future program. Here you have the opportunity of owning a champion, usually in the two- to five-year-old range, which you can enjoy campaigning as a "special" (for Best of Breed competition) and which will be a settled, handsome dog for you and your family to enjoy with pride.

If you are planning foundation for a future kennel, concentrate on acquiring one or two really superior bitches. These need not necessarily be top show-quality, but they should represent your breed's finest producing bloodlines from a strain noted for producing quality, generation after generation. A proven matron who is already the dam of

150

show-type puppies is, of course, the ideal selection; but these are usually difficult to obtain, no one being anxious to part with so valuable an asset. You just might strike it lucky, though, in which case you are off to a flying start. If you cannot find such a matron available, select a young bitch of finest background from top producing lines who is herself of decent type, free of obvious faults, and of good quality.

Great attention should be paid to the pedigree of the bitch from whom you intend to breed. If not already known to you, try to see the sire and dam. It is generally agreed that someone starting with a breed should concentrate on a fine collection of top-flight bitches and raise a few litters from these before considering keeping one's own stud dog. The practice of buying a stud and then breeding everything you own or acquire to that dog does not always work out well. It is better to take advantage of the many noted sires who are available to be used at stud, who represent all of the leading strains, and in each case carefully to select the one who in type and pedigree seems most compatible to each of your bitches, at least for your first several litters.

To summarize, if you want a "family dog" as a companion, it is best to buy it young and raise it to the habits of your household. If you are buying a show dog, the more mature it is, the more certain you can be of its future beauty. If you are buying foundation stock for a kennel, then bitches are better, but they must be from the finest *producing* bloodlines.

When you buy a pure-bred dog that you are told is eligible for registration with the American Kennel Club, you are entitled to receive from the seller an application form which will enable you to register your dog. If the seller cannot give you the application form you should demand and receive an identification of your dog consisting of the name of the breed, the registered names and numbers of the sire and dam, the name of the breeder, and your dog's date of birth. If the litter of which your dog is a part is already recorded with the American Kennel Club, then the litter number is sufficient identification.

Do not be misled by promises of papers at some later date. Demand a registration application form or proper identification as described above. If neither is supplied, do not buy the dog. So warns the American Kennel Club, and this is especially important in the purchase of show or breeding stock.

Crunchie Granola (Ch. Dusten's Pride 'N' Joy ex Dusten's Flavor D'Lite) going Group 1. Owned by Cindy Attinello and Dusten's Cox.

Ch. Dusten's Second Hand Rose, by Ch. Dusten's Sirloin ex Our Cinnamon Karlee, bred by Kathleen and Kurt Stolzenbach, is owned by Cindy Attinello and Dusten and John Cox. At three months old, this beautiful Chow Chow graced the cover of the *American Kennel Gazette* in May 1982.

← **Overleaf:**
This handsome well-trained baby Chow Chow is Kim-Sha's Red Man Chew, taking Group 1st as Best Non-Sporting puppy at 12 weeks old, on his way to Best Puppy in Match. A son of Jewell's Echo Mingus of Wa-Joy ex Hamon's Blue Denim Jeanie. Owned by Barbara Hamon, Oklahoma City, Oklahoma.

Chapter 10

The Care of Your Puppy

Preparing for Your Puppy's Arrival

The moment you decide to be the new owner of a puppy is not one second too soon to start planning for the puppy's arrival in your home. Both the new family member and you will find the transition period easier if your home is geared in advance for the arrival.

The first things to be prepared are a bed for the puppy and a place where you can pen him up for rest periods. I am a firm believer that every dog should have a crate of its own from the very beginning, so that he will come to know and love it as his special place where he is safe and happy. It is an ideal arrangement, for when you want him to be free, the crate stays open. At other times you can securely latch it and know that the pup is safely out of mischief. If you travel with him, his crate comes along in the car; and, of course, in travelling by plane there is no alternative but to have a carrier for the dog. If you show your dog, you will want him upon occasion to be in a crate a good deal of the day. So from every consideration, a crate is a very sensible and sound investment in your puppy's future safety and happiness and for your own peace of mind.

The crates I recommend are the wooden ones with removable side panels, which are ideal for cold weather (with the panels in place to keep out drafts) and in hot weather (with the panels removed to allow

Overleaf: →
Minsh Me Buddy, son of Ch. Chance by Minsh, grandson of Ch. Don Lee Messiah, great-grandson of Ch. Don Lee's Prophet, great-great grandson of Ch. Beamer's Chummy Chinaman, at one of the match shows where he won. Mrs. Armin Krupp, owner, Minsh Chow Chows, Quebec.

Ch. Shanghai's Cotton Candy, 6 months old, takes a 3-point major under Joseph Rowe at Bryn Mawr in 1980. Bred and owned by K. Jane Weiss, Pottsville, Pennsylvania.

better air circulation). Wire crates are all right in the summer, but they give no protection from cold or drafts. I intensely dislike aluminum crates due to the manner in which aluminum reflects surrounding temperatures. If it is cold, so is the metal of the crate; if it is hot, the crate becomes burning hot. For this reason I consider aluminum crates neither comfortable nor safe.

When you choose the puppy's crate, be certain that it is roomy enough not to become outgrown. The crate should have sufficient height so the dog can stand up in it as a mature dog and sufficient area so that he can stretch out full length when relaxed. When the puppy is young, first give him shredded newspaper as a bed; the papers can be replaced with a mat or turkish towels when the dog is older. Carpet remnants are great for the bottom of the crate, as they are inexpensive and in case of accidents can be quite easily replaced. As the dog matures and is past the chewing age, a pillow or blanket in the crate is an appreciated comfort.

Sharing importance with the crate is a safe area in which the puppy can exercise and play. If you are an apartment dweller, a baby's play-pen for a toy dog or a young puppy works out well; for a larger breed or older puppy use a portable exercise pen which you can then use later when traveling with your dog or for dog shows. If you have a yard, an area where he can be outside in safety should be fenced in prior to the dog's arrival at your home. This area does not need to be huge, but it does need to be made safe and secure. If you are in a suburban area where there are close neighbors, stockade fencing works out best as then the neighbors are less aware of the dog and the dog cannot see and bark at everything passing by. If you are out in the country where no problems with neighbors are likely to occur, then regular chain-link fencing is fine. For added precaution in both cases, use a row of concrete blocks or railroad ties inside against the entire bottom of the fence; this precludes or at least considerably lessens the chances of your dog digging his way out.

Be advised that if yours is a single dog, it is very unlikely that it will get sufficient exercise just sitting in the fenced area, which is what most of them do when they are there alone. Two or more dogs will play and move themselves around, but from my own experience, one by itself does little more than make a leisurely tour once around the area to check things over and then lie down. You must include a daily walk or two in your plans if your puppy is to be rugged and well. Exercise is extremely important to a puppy's muscular development and to

A handsome head-study of Can. Ch. Minsh Darleen owned by Mrs. Armin Krupp, Minsh Kennels, St. Eustache, Quebec, Canada.

keep a mature dog fit and trim. So make sure that those exercise periods, or walks, a game of ball, and other such activities, are part of your daily program as a dog owner.

If your fenced area has an outside gate, provide a padlock and key and a strong fastening for it, and use them, so that the gate can not be opened by others and the dog taken or turned free. The ultimate con-

Ch. Dusten's Almond Joy at 3 months old winning the Non-Sporting Group at an important match show event. Dusten and John Cox, owners, Sharon, Conn.

IN SHOW

YGAN KC

1, 1983

oto by

Photography

BEST IN SHOW

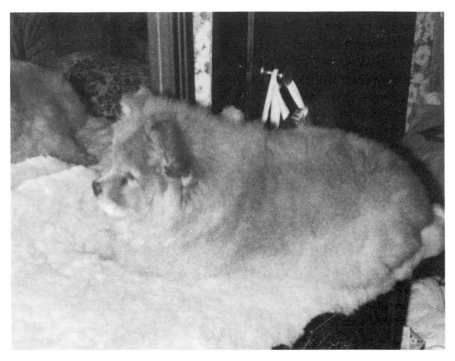

An adorable 14 weeks-old Chow puppy, Golden Nugget, in November 1979. Owned by Mr. and Mrs. Maurice Lacroix, Bromont, P.Q., Canada.

venience in this regard is, of course, a door (unused for other purposes) from the house around which the fenced area can be enclosed, so that all you have to do is open the door and out into his area he goes. This arrangement is safest of all, as then you need not be using a gate, and it is easier in bad weather since then you can send the dog out without taking him and becoming soaked yourself at the same time. This is not always possible to manage, but if your house is arranged so that you could do it this way, I am sure you would never regret it due to the convenience and added safety thus provided. Fencing in the entire yard, with gates to be opened and closed whenever a caller, deliveryman, postman, or some other person comes on your property, really is not safe at all because people not used to gates and their importance are frequently careless about closing and latching gates

← **Overleaf:**
Ch. Charkay's Grand Marnier O'Palm, by Ch. Charkay's Lord Calvert O'Palm ex Ch. Charkay's Creme Chablis O'Palm, was bred by K.L. Porter and Mae Palm and is co-owned by K. Porter and M. Schneider of Brazil. This dog, handled by Ken Murray, is a consistent and widely admired Group and Best in Show winner.

securely. I know of many heartbreaking incidents brought about by someone carelessly only half closing a gate which the owner had thought to be firmly latched and the dog wandering out. For greatest security a fenced *area* definitely takes precedence over a fenced *yard*.

The puppy will need a collar (one that fits now, not one to be grown into) and lead from the moment you bring him home. Both should be an appropriate weight and type for his size. Also needed are a feeding dish and a water dish, both made preferably of unbreakable material. Your pet supply shop should have an interesting assortment of these and other accessories from which you can choose. Then you will need grooming tools of the type the breeder recommends and some toys. One of the best toys is a beef bone, either rib, leg, or knuckle (the latter the type you can purchase to make soup), cut to an appropriate size for your puppy dog. These are absolutely safe and are great exercise for the teething period, helping to get the baby teeth quickly out of the

Minsh Me Buddy at five months. A son of Chance by Minsh, grandson of Minsh Cia and Ch. Don Lee's Messiah, and great-grandson of Ch. Don Lee's Prophet. A puppy of exciting potential owned by Mrs. Armin Krupp, St. Eustache, Quebec, Canada.

Ch. Shanghai's Memory's of Meme, Best of Opposite Sex from the classes under Henry Stoecker at Boardwalk Kennel Club 1981. Bred by K. Jane Weiss, Pottsville, Pennsylvania.

Opposite page: *(Top)* Mrs. Barbara Durst, owner of Sunswept Chow Chows, with her great homebred Am. and Can. Ch. Sunswept Tonka. *(Bottom)* Laura Perkinson, owner of Taichung Chow Chows at Olympia, Washington, with 3 of her favorites. *Left,* Taichung Samantha, by Leatherwood Kadiz ex Taichung Tabatha; *center,* Taichung Dark Design, by Ch. Plainacres Black Smoke ex Huns Chows Hannah; *right,* Taichung Justin of Mike-Mar, by Ch. Kobys Casanova of Sweetkins ex Teabear's Dewberry Well.

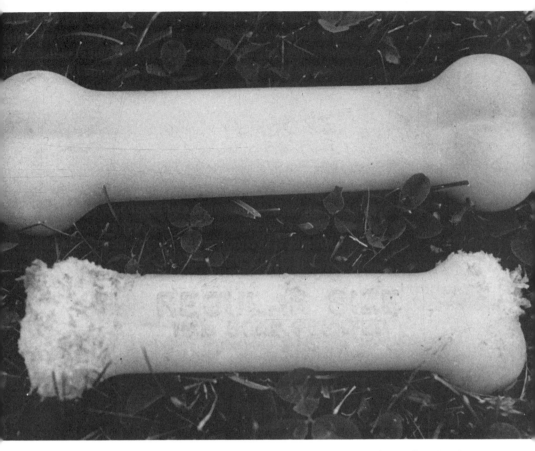

The tasty meat flavor of Nylabone® is enjoyed by any breed of dog. Get the size compatible with your Chow's age. It serves as a chew toy, helps clean the teeth, and can be used as a training device, too. Photo by Vince Serbin.

way with no problems. Equally satisfactory is Nylabone® , a nylon bone that does not chip or splinter and that "frizzles" as the puppy chews, providing healthful gum massage. Rawhide chews are safe, too, *IF made in the United States.* There was a problem a few years back owing to the chemicals with which some foreign rawhide toys had been treated, since which time we have carefully avoided giving them to our own dogs. Also avoid plastics and any sort of rubber toys, *particularly* those with squeakers which the puppy may remove and swallow. If you want a ball for the puppy to use when playing with him, select one of very hard construction made for this purpose and do not leave it alone with him because he may chew off and swallow bits of the rubber. Take the ball with you when the game is over. This also applies to some of those "tug of war" type rubber toys which are fun when used with the two of you for that purpose but again should *not* be left behind for the dog to work on with his teeth. Bits of swallowed rubber, squeakers, and other such foreign articles can wreak great havoc in the intestinal tract—do all you can to guard against them.

Too many changes all at once can be difficult for a puppy. For at least the first few days he is with you, keep him on the food and feeding schedule to which he is accustomed. Find out ahead of time from the breeder what he feeds his puppies, how frequently, and at what times of the day. Also find out what, if any, food supplements the breeder has been using and recommends. Then be prepared by getting in a supply of the same food so that you will have it there when you bring the puppy home. Once the puppy is accustomed to his new surroundings, then you can switch the type of food and schedule to fit your convenience, but for the first several days do it as the puppy expects.

Your selection of a veterinarian also should be attended to before the puppy comes home, because you should stop at the vet's office for the puppy to be checked over as soon as you leave the breeder's premises. If the breeder is from your area, ask him for recommendations. Ask your dog-owning friends for their opinions of the local veterinarians, and see what their experiences with those available have been. Choose someone whom several of your friends recommend highly, then contact him about your puppy, perhaps making an appointment to stop in at his office. If the premises are clean, modern, and well equipped, and if you like the veterinarian, make an appointment to bring the puppy in on the day of purchase. Be sure to obtain the puppy's health record from the breeder, including information on such things as shots and worming that the puppy has had.

Joining the Family

Remember that, exciting and happy an occasion as it is for you, the puppy's move from his place of birth to your home can be, for him, a traumatic experience. His mother and littermates will be missed. He quite likely will be awed or frightened by the change of surroundings. The person on whom he depended will be gone. Everything should be planned to make his arrival at your home pleasant—to give him confidence and to help him realize that yours is a pretty nice place to be after all.

Ch. Jen-Sens China Bear of Palm, owned by Desmond J. Murphy, Mae Palm and
Stonybrook Kennels, handled by Mr. Murphy to Group 1. Alexander Schwartz, judge.

Ch. Sweetkins of Albelarm, by Ch. Checkmate's Nickelodean ex Sweetkins China Syndrome, pictured at 13 months. Bred by Art and Barbara Friedman. Owned by Mrs. Alan Robson and Michael Wolf.

Never bring a puppy home on a holiday. There just is too much going on with people and gifts and excitement. If he is in honor of an "occasion," work it out so that his arrival will be a few days earlier or, perhaps even better, a few days later than the "occasion." Then your home will be back to its normal routine and the puppy can enjoy your undivided attention. Try not to bring the puppy home in the evening. Early morning is the ideal time, as then he has the opportunity of getting acquainted and the initial strangeness should wear off before bedtime. You will find it a more peaceful night that way, I am sure. Allow the puppy to investigate as he likes, under your watchful eye. If you already have a pet in the household, keep a careful watch that the relationship between the two gets off to a friendly start or you may quickly find yourself with a lasting problem. Much of the future attitude of each toward the other will depend on what takes place that first day, so keep your mind on what they are doing and let your other activities slide for the moment. Be careful not to let your older pet become jealous by paying more attention to the puppy than to him, as that will start a bad situation immediately.

If you have a child, here again it it important that the relationship start out well. Before the puppy is brought home, you should have a talk with the youngster about puppies, so that it will be clearly understood that puppies are fragile and can easily be injured; therefore, they should not be teased, hurt, mauled, or overly rough-housed. A puppy is not an inanimate toy; it is a living thing with a right to be loved and handled respectfully, treatment which will reflect in the dog's attitude toward your child as both mature together. Never permit your children's playmates to mishandle the puppy, as I have seen happen, tormenting the puppy until it turns on the children in self-defense. Children often do not realize how rough is too rough. You, as a responsible adult, are obligated to assure that your puppy's relationship with children is a pleasant one.

Do not start out by spoiling your puppy. A puppy is usually pretty smart and can be quite demanding. What you had considered to be "just for tonight" may be accepted by the puppy as "for keeps." Be firm with him, strike a routine, and stick to it. The puppy will learn more quickly this way, and everyone will be happier at the result. A radio playing softly or a dim night light are often comforting to a puppy as it gets accustomed to new surroundings and should be provided in preference to bringing the puppy to bed with you—unless, of course, you intend him to share the bed as a permanent arrangement.

170

A tisket, a tasket, a baby Chow with her basket! Ch. Dusten's Second Hand Rose, personality puppy par excellence, at three months old. Owned by Cindy Attinello and Dusten Cox, Rose is a daughter of Ch. Dusten's Sirloin and was bred by Kathleen and Karl Stolzenbach.

Ch. Dusten's Big Shot Casey, by Dusten's Dudley Do Right ex Ky-Lin Ethyl, handled by John Cox for himself and Dusten Cox, Dusten's Chow Chows, Sharon, Connecticut.

Socializing the Chow Chow
by Desmond J. Murphy

Desmond J. Murphy has been a Chow fancier for many years, and his experiences with the breed have taught him the enormous importance of socialization. *A.K.N.*

Many experienced Chowists believe that a good Chow temperament is related more to environment than to heredity; that is, "nurture" is more important than "nature." If the environment, indeed, is of such paramount importance, the puppy's environment must be extended so that he is able not only to accept members of his own household but also strangers and foreign situations. In short, a Chow puppy must be socialized. Many years ago, in the 1920's and 1930's, many Chows did exhibit a "sharp" temperament. The biggest reasons for that kind of anti-social behavior was the lack of understanding about socialization as a part of dog psychology. Today, we have made advances in that regard, and everyone agrees that a Chow must be socialized. According to one authority in Chows, "Socialization is the process by which the Chow puppy is taught to meet and like human beings, other dogs, different environments from his own home, and other foreign situations, with steadiness, calm, and even affability."

The socialization process generally consists of 16 steps.

1. Begin to pick up the Chow puppy when he is about a week old, that is, before he has his eyes open. Pet him gently and talk to him softly. Although he may cry at first, he will eventually like being held and talked to.

2. Pick up the puppy every day. When his eyes open, he will adjust through his visual perception to being held.

3. When strangers come to call, ask them to hold the puppy. Pick up the puppy carefully and place him in the hands of your guest. If you can, invite a few friends to visit you, so they, too, may assist you in this "socialization" process.

4. When the puppy begins to walk, play with him gently. As he grows older, romp with him, and pick him up often so that he likes the idea of being lifted into your arms. Sometimes young Chows do not like to be picked up, but if that action is accompanied with praise and a hug, he will accustom himself to being picked up.

Kids love Chow pups, too! The one on the *left* is now Can. Ch. Minsh Cia, the dam of Can. Ch. Chance by Minsh being hugged by owner Mrs. Armin Krupp's oldest son.

Canada's most famous Chow Chow, Can. and Am. Ch. Mi Tu's Han Su Shang, born Dec. 1972, by Ch. Foo H'Sing's Mister Lin Wu ex Ch. Chi Kwang's Han Su Mei, has broken all records for the breed in Canada and boasts a fine array of U.S. successes as well. Bred by Mr. and Mrs. H. Robb, "Shang" is head man at the Bu-Dynasty Kennels owned by Mr. and Mrs. Herb Williams and Mr. J.C.F. Peddie of Ontario. Mr. Williams is handling under judge Anna Katherine Nicholas.

5. As soon as the puppy has had the first shots, start to take him in the car with you when you go on short errands. Take the puppy out of the car and if a stranger is interested and willing, let the stranger hold the puppy.

6. Start putting the puppy on the grooming table when he is a couple of weeks old—after he has opened his eyes. Begin to open his mouth regularly, for some Chows do not like to oblige in that regard. Praise the puppy warmly as he opens his mouth. Make this "opening" a little game so that he will come to enjoy showing his teeth and pigment.

7. If your Chow is a male, begin to touch his rear end frequently and his testicles. Run your hand up and down his rear legs, and in the buttocks area as well, so that the puppy will get used to being touched in the rear. This touching process also may be treated as a game in which you praise him highly when he is amenable to being touched in that area.

8. Whenever you go to visit friends, take your puppy with you. By the age of three months, if you have done your "socialization" work properly, he should not be shy with strangers. In fact, he should welcome meeting people. Sometimes a Chow is perfectly well adjusted to his home environment, but when he is put into a "foreign" place, he may lower his tail and become afraid. Such fear may come from the Chow's acute sense of "smelling"—centuries ago in China he was used as a hunting dog. In any case, take the puppy to as many strange environments as you can so that he easily adjusts to new smells and new places.

9. Take your puppy to any public place where people gather and where dogs are allowed. Children often will volunteer to pet your Chow. Provided the puppy has been trained not to snap or bite, ask the children to kneel down or bend over and pet the puppy *under the chin first.* That affectionate touching may be the antidote for shyness, if the puppy, for whatever reason, has become "head shy." Let the children pick up the puppy if they want to, as you stand guard to see that they do not drop the puppy. Of course, common sense would dictate that you cannot take your puppy to a public place where automobiles arrive in great numbers—unless the puppy has been lead broken. (The Chow puppy can be taught to walk on a lead at the early age of six weeks.)

10. A good test for you to make in regard to your puppy's success as to socialization is the following: whenever you take your puppy to a public place or any new environment, look at his tail. If he puts his tail down, that is the sure signal that he is uncomfortable and insecure. Pet

Jade with two of her babies, all three of them cinnamon, and her owner Marilyn Short, AHSO Fan-C Chow Chows, Wichita, Kansas.

K. Jane Weiss, owner of Shanghai Chows, with her best buddy, Ch. Shanghai's Enie Minie Mighty Mo. Such a very handsome dog!

Ch. Shanghai Mastradomas owner-handled here by Marilyn Short to Winners Dog under Wilma Hunter at Hutchinson Kennel Club.

Opposite page: Ch. Marian's Imperial Pandy Bear in June 1981 handled by John Reife.

Am. and Can. Ch. Sunswept Tonka listens attentively to the story being shared by him with his owner's granddaughter, Kate Talkington. Barbara Durst, Sunswept Chows, Parkton, Maryland.

him and reassure him. Give him an extra hug and get him to feel that the new environment will be fun and secure. If you have done your socialization work properly, his tail should fall down only briefly, not for the entire visit to the new place. If you have been totally successful, the puppy's tail will never fall down, or drop.

11. If a puppy becomes really angry at his brothers and sisters and is not just "roughhousing" with them, the offending puppy who wishes to bite his peers must be removed and kept separate from the others.

12. Chow puppies should be introduced to other puppies when the litter is about three months old. At this age, it is a good idea to enter a match show. The puppy should enjoy meeting all the other puppies and strangers as he goes through this first experience at a dog show. If you have done your work well, he should be content and at ease. By now he is lead broken, table trained, experienced at opening his mouth and if a male, having his testes touched by the judge.

13. Importantly, you should continue to socialize your Chow in every way possible. He should like both children and adults and should be amenable to being touched by complete strangers.

14. If your Chow should regress in regard to socialization, do not blame him. Blame yourself. Some Chows' temperaments are set early concerning affability and some take longer. If the Chow exhibits

"social problems," begin the socialization process over again. Whatever happens, do not allow your Chow to be "anti-social," a potential ruination of the breed.

15. The socialization process as described above is not only for Chows which will be shown but also for *all* Chow Chows. An unfriendly or aggressive Chow is a grave liability for the Chow breed and such a temperament cannot be allowed.

16. A Chow which is "socialized" is well adjusted, happy, and he has no psychological hang-ups or problems. He is amenable to being handled by strangers in and out of the ring, and no new environment or situation frightens him. He is a happy Chow in being well adjusted; and because of your belief in the socialized Chow, he is a more pleasant animal and you are a more relaxed, happy owner.

Nothing is more important than the socialization of the Chow Chow, and this idea should become the heart of the Chowist philosophy.

This darling baby Chow is Biddle's Tribute to Shawnee, owned by Shanghai Chows, K. Jane Weiss, Pottsville, Pennsylvania.

Overleaf: →
Ch. Kitts Macho Man, born November 1981, by Ch. Cedar Creek Shannee ex Cedar Creek Miss Muffet. Macho Man and his dam both owned by K. Jane Weiss, Shanghai Chows, Pottsville, Pennsylvania.

Two-and-a-half weeks-old Chow puppy—a future "star" at Dusten's Kennels, Dusten and John Cox, Sharon, Connecticut.

Training Your New Puppy

The training of your puppy should start the very day of his arrival in your home. Never address him without calling him by name. A short, simple name is the easiest to teach as it catches the dog's attention quickly, so avoid elaborate call names. Always address the dog by the same name, not a whole series of pet names; the latter will only confuse the puppy.

Using his name clearly, call the puppy over to you when you see him awake and wandering about. When he comes, make a big fuss over him for being such a good dog. He thus will quickly associate the sound of his name with coming to you and a pleasant happening.

Several hours after the puppy's arrival is not too soon to start accustoming him to the feel of a light collar. He may hardly notice it; or he may struggle, roll over, and try to rub it off his neck with his paws. Divert his attention when this occurs by offering a tasty snack or a toy

← **Overleaf:**
Can. Ch. Chinabear Waggin' Master, by Am. and Can. Ch. Cabaret's King of Hearts ex Am. and Can. Ch. Cherie's Firewind Fiesta. Bred by Gary and Carmen Blankenship. Owned by Marge Ste. Marie, Brossard, P.Q., Canada.

186

(starting a game with him) or by petting him. Before long he will have accepted the strange feeling around his neck and no longer appear aware of it. Next comes the lead. Attach it and then immediately take the puppy outside or otherwise try to divert his attention with things to see and sniff. He may struggle against the lead at first, biting at it and trying to free himself. Do not pull him with it at this point; just hold the end loosely and try to follow him if he starts off in any direction. Normally his attention will soon turn to investigating his surroundings if he is outside or you have taken him into an unfamiliar room in your house; curiosity will take over and he will become interested in sniffing around the surroundings. Just follow him with the lead slackly held until he seems to have completely forgotten about it;

This stunning eight-week-old puppy is already in training for his show career. Future Can. Ch. Bo-Bleu of Chenango strikes a perfect pose at the end of his lead. Lucille Joly, owner, Pincourt, P.Q., Canada.

Ch. Don-Lee Chowtime, owned by Desmond J. Murphy and Susie Donnelly, at Ramapo 1980. Mr. Murphy handling; R. William Taylor the judge.

Opposite page: *(Top)* Ch. Ro Don's Buddy X Lin Su is a grandson of Ch. Ro Don's Mr. Chips. In less than a year's showing he has won 7 Bests in Show along with 30 Group firsts. Owned by Ron Ewing. Handled by Ken Rensink. Anna Katherine Nicholas, judge. *(Bottom)* The Wu Li Maestro by Bu Dynasty's Heavy Duty ex Ch. Lorraine's Skarlet of Samchow, taking Best of Breed at Heart of America Kennel Club 1983 under judge Frank Oberstar. Meribeth Correll, breeder-owner.

189

This fabulous puppy, owned by Dusten Cox, is Champion Dusten's Ex Cedrin, by Ch. Car Mar Pucker for Dusten. Dusten's Chows, Sharon, Connecticut.

then try with gentle urging to get him to follow you. Don't be rough or jerk at him; just tug gently on the lead in short quick motions (steady pulling can become a battle of wills), repeating his name or trying to get him to follow your hand which is holding a bit of food or an interesting toy. If you have an older lead-trained dog, then it should be a cinch to get the puppy to follow along after *him*. In any event, the average puppy learns quite quickly and will soon be trotting along nicely on the lead. Once that point has been reached, the next step is to teach him to follow on your left side, or heel. Of course this will not likely be accomplished all in one day but should be done with short training periods over the course of several days until you are satisfied with the result.

During the course of house training your puppy, you will need to take him out frequently and at regular intervals: first thing in the morning directly from the crate, immediately after meals, after the puppy has been napping, or when you notice that the puppy is looking for a spot. Choose more or less the same place to take the puppy each time so that a pattern will be established. If he does not go immediately, do not return him to the house as he will probably relieve himself the moment he is inside. Stay out with him until he has finished; then be lavish with your praise for his good behavior. If you catch the puppy having an accident indoors, grab him firmly and rush him outside, sharply saying "No!" as you pick him up. If you do not see the accident occur, there is little point in doing anything except cleaning it up, as once it has happened and been forgotten, the puppy will most likely not even realize why you are scolding him.

With a medium-sized breed as a chow, especially if you live in a big city or are away many hours at a time, having a dog that is trained to go on paper has some very definite advantages. To do this, one proceeds pretty much the same way as taking the puppy outdoors, except now you place the puppy on the newspaper at the proper time. The paper should always be kept in the same spot. An easy way to paper train a puppy if you have a playpen for it or an exercise pen is to line the area with newspapers; then gradually, every day or so, remove a section of newspaper until you are down to just one or two. The puppy acquires the habit of using the paper; and as the prepared area grows smaller, in the majority of cases the dog will continue to use whatever paper is still available. My own experience is that this works out well. It is pleasant, if the dog is alone for an excessive length of time, to be able to feel that if he needs it the paper is there and will be used.

The puppy should form the habit of spending a certain amount of time in his crate, even when you are home. Sometimes the puppy will do this voluntarily, but if not it should be taught to do so, which is accomplished by leading the puppy over by his collar, gently pushing him inside, and saying firmly "Down" or "Stay." Whatever expression you use to give a command, stick to the very same one each time for each act. Repetition is the big thing in training—and so is association with what the dog is expected to do. When you mean "Sit" always say exactly that. "Stay" should mean *only* that the dog should remain where he receives the command. "Down" means something else again. Do not confuse the dog by shuffling the commands, as this will create training problems for you.

GOLDEN STATE ~~~ CHOW CLUB

Feeding Your Dog

Time was when providing nourishing food for our dogs involved a far more complicated procedure than people now feel is necessary. The old school of thought was that the daily ration must consist of fresh beef, vegetables, cereal, egg yolks, and cottage cheese as basics with such additions as brewer's yeast and vitamin tablets on a daily basis.

During recent years, however, many minds have changed regarding this procedure. We still give eggs, cottage cheese, and supplements to the diet, but the basic method of feeding dogs has changed; and the change has been, in the opinion of many authorities, definitely for the better. The school of thought now is that you are doing your dogs a favor when you feed them some of the fine commercially prepared dog foods in preference to your own home-cooked concoctions.

The reason behind this new outlook is easily understandable. The dog food industry has grown to be a major one, participated in by some of the best known and most respected names in the American way of life. These trusted firms, it is agreed, turn out excellent products, so people are feeding their dog food preparations with confidence and the dogs are thriving, living longer, happier, and healthier lives than ever before. What more could we want?

There are at least half a dozen absolutely top-grade dry foods to be mixed with broth or water and served to your dog according to directions. There are all sorts of canned meats, and there are several kinds of "convenience foods," those in a packet which you open and dump out into the dog's dish. It is just that simple. The "convenience" foods are neat and easy to use when you are away from home, but generally speaking we prefer a dry food mixed with hot water or soup and meat. We also feel that the canned meat, with its added fortifiers, is more beneficial to the dogs than the fresh meat. However, the two can be alternated or, if you prefer and your dog does well on it, by all means use fresh ground beef. A dog enjoys changes in the meat part of his diet, which is easy with the canned food since all sorts of beef are available (chunk, ground, stewed, and so on), plus lamb, chicken, and

Opposite page: Ch. Cabaret Crackerjack, C.D., by Ch. Cabaret Blackjack ex Cabaret Royal Flush, taking Best in Sweepstakes at Golden State Chow Chow Club, April 1979, under judge Mr. Takagi of Japan. Bred and owned by Joan and James Richard, Cabaret Chows. Jamie Richard handling.

even such concoctions as liver and egg, just plain liver flavor, and a blend of five meats.

There also is prepared food geared to every age bracket of your dog's life, from puppyhood on through old age, with special additions or modifications to make it particularly nourishing and beneficial. Our grandparents, and even our parents, never had it so good where the canine dinner is concerned, because these commercially prepared foods are tasty and geared to meeting the dog's gastronomic approval.

Additionally, contents and nutrients are clearly listed on the labels, as are careful instructions for feeding just the right amount for the size, weight, and age of each dog.

With these foods we do not feel the addition of extra vitamins is necessary, but if you do there are several kinds of those, too, that serve as taste treats as well as being beneficial. Your pet supplier has a full array of them.

Of course there is no reason not to cook up something for your dog if you would feel happier doing so. But it seems to us unnecessary when such truly satisfactory rations are available with so much less trouble and expense.

How often you feed your dog is a matter of how it works out best for you. Many owners prefer to do it once a day. I personally think that two meals, each of smaller quantity, are better for the digestion and more satisfying to the dog, particularly if yours is a household member who stands around and watches preparations for the family meals. Do not overfeed. That is the shortest route to all sorts of problems. Follow directions and note carefully how your dog is looking. If your dog is overweight, cut back the quantity of food a bit. If the dog looks thin, then increase the amount. Each dog is an individual and the food intake should be adjusted to his requirements to keep him feeling and looking trim and in top condition.

From the time puppies are fully weaned until they are about twelve weeks old, they should be fed four times daily. From three months to six months of age, three meals should suffice. At six months of age the puppies can be fed two meals, and the twice daily feedings can be continued until the puppies are close to one year old, at which time feeding can be changed to once daily if desired.

If you do feed just once a day, do so by early afternoon at the latest and give the dog a snack, or biscuit or two, at bedtime.

Remember that plenty of fresh water should always be available to your puppy or dog for drinking. This is of utmost importance to his health.

Ch. Shanghai's Enie Minie Mighty Mo now fully grown and a famous winner taking points towards his title in 1981 under Dr. Leon Seligman. Owned by K. Jane Weiss, Pottsville, Pennsylvania.

Ch. Don-Lee Chowtime, owned by Desmond Murphy and Susie Donnelly, relaxes in regal dignity on his grooming table, waiting to be taken into the ring.

Chapter 11

Correct Grooming and Bathing of Your Chow

By Desmond J. Murphy

One of the Chow Chow's most distinctive and beautiful features is his coat which, in the words of the standard, should be "abundant, dense, straight and off-standing; rather coarse in texture, with a soft, woolly undercoat." The care of this coat requires very special "know how" if the dog is to be kept at his best, and we can think of no one better qualified to describe exactly how it should be done than Desmond J. Murphy, noted breeder-owner-handler and now a judge, who is widely admired for his expert presentation of his Chows, and for the immaculate, gleaming, well-conditioned appearance of their coats.

Since this is a breed which will need grooming at every age, the earlier you accustom your Chow to the routine the easier it will be for you as he matures. So do start off soon as you acquire your puppy, even if he is to be solely a pet, so that he will grow up to be a well groomed, handsome source of pride around your home.

Mr. Murphy is a consistent exhibitor who almost invariably handles his own dogs, and who conditions and cares for their coats personally. The expertise with which he does so speaks for itself when one considers the steady succession of Best in Group and Best in Show awards they bring home!

We are very proud to present you with the following chapter on coat care in which Mr. Murphy shares his "secrets for success" with you. We feel that in writing it he has made a major contribution to the value of this book. *A.K.N.*

Grooming the Adult

Chow Chows must be groomed for the sake of good health and, of course, for the show ring. Although one may frequently hear that a Chow does not have to be bathed very often, that idea is false. The Chow must be bathed regularly and groomed often if he is to be kept in healthy, tip-top condition. Many Chowists believe that "hot spots" (creeping eczema) often begin when a Chow's coat is dirty and matted. This negligence often results in the dog's itching, scratching, and even biting the skin. Whatever the cause of "hot spots," they are minimized in a Chow which is bathed and groomed regularly. In regard to presenting a Chow properly in the show ring, several articles have been written by Chow judges deploring the dirty, unkempt Chows which are frequently seen in the ring. A dirty Chow in the show ring should not be tolerated. Therefore, two strong reasons exist for bathing and grooming your Chow: the dog's health and his proper appearance in the show ring.

The following equipment is useful in grooming the Chow Chow:
1. A professional grooming table.
2. A wire slicker or "rake."
3. A "pin" brush, often referred to as a "Poodle brush."
4. A steel comb.
5. A pair of nail clippers or an electric nail grinder.
6. A pair of scissors.
7. Some commercial coat conditioner in a spray bottle or aerosol can.

Possible Grooming Positions

The best grooming position is the "lying" position, the dog's middle piece and stomach being accessible from this prone position. An adult Chow, which has never been trained to lie on its side, rarely can be taught this position as an adult. Teaching the Chow to lie on its side should be done as a very young puppy, as young as six weeks, perhaps. Two more positions which are useful are the "full-standing" position and the "sitting" position, both being natural even to the Chow that has not been trained to lie on its side.

Brushing the Chow "to the skin"

1. Place the Chow in the "lying" position or in the standing position if he has not been trained to lie on the grooming table. Use the pin brush to part the Chow's coat to the skin at the withers, the "part" be-

Ch. Shanghai's Memory's of Meme (cinnamon), by Cedar Creek Charlie Brown ex Ch. Cedar Creek's Party Girl, being groomed at Boardwalk Kennel Club, standing on the rubber-topped grooming table for last minute touches. K. Jane Weiss, breeder-owner, Shanghai Chows, Pottsville, Pennsylvania.

ing perpendicular to the dog's length of body and to the grooming table. The part is made from the withers to the underside of the rib cage.

2. Brush along the part—from the skin to the end of the guard hairs. Brush to the right of the part and to the left of the part using as much coat conditioner as is needed. The pink of the Chow's skin is always visible during this "brush to the skin" process.

3. After brushing to the skin along this long part for ten to fifteen minutes (or more if you have the patience), move the part toward the Chow's rear end and rear legs about ¼ inch to ½ inch. Brush again along the part—from the skin to the end of the guard hairs. Brush to the right of the part and to the left of the part using as much coat conditioner as is needed. Again, the skin of the Chow should be easily visible.

4. After brushing to the skin along this part for several minutes, then move the part, once again, toward the rear of the dog about ¼ to ½ inch. Continue to brush along this new part as suggested in directions two and three.

5. When one has reached the rear of the Chow, return to the middle of the dog and begin the "part and brush" method, moving the part toward the head of the dog. This parting toward the head will, of course, necessitate the groomer's moving to the other side of the grooming table, that is, if the groomer is right-handed. For the right-handed groomer, most of the brushing is done toward the "right" of the part.

199

Final touches for Am., Can., and Bda. Ch. Jen Jen O'Cambellyn, noted Alaskan Chow Chow, owned by Phyllis Castleton, Anchorage, Alaska.

6. Finish the grooming of one entire side of the Chow following the instructions above. Then the Chow must be turned over so that the same process may begin on the ungroomed side.

7. After the Chow's middle piece is brushed thoroughly, then brush the legs, the tail, the pants, the ruff, and the top of the head, and the front. The method of parting and brushing to the skin may also be used for the above anatomical parts, the brushing of which may be done with the dog in the standing or sitting position.

8. Since most of the grooming done thus far has been done with the pin brush, the groomer may wish to change to the "slicker" or "rake" to take out any mats on the skull or behind the ears where the coat is usually softer than that of the body.

9. The "standing" position should be used to put on the finishing touches. All the hair of the body, tail, and ruff should be brushed forward to give a look of polish and finish. Brushing the Chow's ruff forward gives the "leonine" or "lion-like" look often associated with the Chow. The official Chow standard reads "accentuated by a ruff. . . clothed in a shining, offstanding coat, the Chow is a masterpiece of beauty, dignity, and untouched naturalness." These breed characteristics are heightened by the thorough and time-consuming grooming described here.

10. Since every hair on the Chow has been brushed to the skin, even further finishing touches may be added by using a steel comb whose teeth measure from 1/4 to 1/8 inches apart. The steel comb will further accentuate the look of "every hair has been brushed to the skin."

11. Be sure the Chow's eyes are clean, and if there is any tearing that wets the muzzle, be sure to dry the muzzle shortly before going into the show ring. Also do not forget to cut off the long guard hairs on the Chow's feet with a pair of barber's scissors. Rounding off the Chow's feet so that they appear compact, round, and cat-like is permissible and is done by even the most conservative Chowist. *However, excessive trimming of the Chow's belly coat or coat anywhere except on the feet should not be done, for the standard stresses that the Chow is a masterpiece of "untouched naturalness."*

12. Now that the Chow is groomed to perfection, and is ready to step into the ring, you may well feel proud of the accomplishment. Bathing and grooming the Chow thoroughly is most time-consuming. Some expert Chow groomers and professional Chow handlers indicate that from tub to show ring may take as long as six hours. It is no wonder that the perfectly groomed Chow often wins over the Chow which is dirty, strong-smelling, and unbrushed. If you have accomplished this excellent grooming, you can give yourself a pat on the back and an extra hug to your Chow for having been so patient. In the end, your Chow will be a healthier animal and a winning one—if he is properly groomed.

Grooming the Puppy

The Chow puppy can be groomed by using the "slicker" or "wire rake" rather than the pin brush. The puppy can be groomed in exactly the same manner as the adult Chow. It is a distinct advantage to begin the grooming of the Chow puppy when he is from four to six weeks old.

At that young age, one can more easily teach the puppy to lie on its side. Place the puppy on his side on a grooming table or a card table if you do not yet own a grooming table. Pet him gently on his side, rub his tummy, and tell him what a wonderful puppy he is. At first, insist that he lie on his side for only a minute, then increase the time gradually until he can relax, lying still for five minutes, then ten, until he can be comfortable there for twenty minutes to a half-hour, perhaps. You must stay with him; you may, of course, be seated on a chair next to the table while teaching him this procedure. He will learn to like lying on his side because he will associate this method with the good feeling of being petted and rubbed on his tummy, and with kind, verbal praise. How grateful you will be to yourself for having taken the time when the puppy is young to teach him this valuable position. Grooming him in this lying position is by far the easiest and most successful in accomplishing excellent "to the skin" grooming.

When the Chow is a little baby of two or three weeks, you should trim his toenails with human manicure scissors; then later on, you can introduce a rotary grinder or professional dog nail clippers. If a puppy is introduced to the rather sharp noise of the rotary grinder at an early age, for brief periods of time, he will get used to the noise gradually. Because Chows are particularly sensitive to having their toenails cut, many Chowists have found the rotary grinder to be an effective method of keeping the nails short. Some, of course, have success with the nail clippers. Whatever method is used, the Chow from an early age should be exposed to having his nails ground or clipped.

Bathing

For the general health of your Chow and for his presentation in the show ring, the Chow should be bathed. Depending on how dirty he gets from his living conditions (inside a kennel, in the house, or in a gravel or dirt run), the Chow should be bathed when he gets dirty.

Equipment and Supplies Needed

You'll need some kind of dryer. A commercial dryer is best, although in a pinch a ladies' hair dryer may be used instead. You'll also need shampoo, a rubber mat for the tub, several bath towels, some mineral oil and cotton balls, and a hand spray or length of hose.

Procedure for Bathing

1. Place a rubber mat, a piece of carpet, or even two towels on the bottom of the tub to keep the dog from slipping. Put some mineral oil in each eye to prevent any burning from the soap suds. Put some cotton in each of his ears to prevent water from entering the ears. These cotton ear plugs may also lessen the sound of the dryer if your Chow is sensitive to it.

2. Use warm water. Start wetting the Chow at the withers with the hose and work backward to the end of the tail. The head should be wet last.

3. When the coat is completely soaked with warm water, work up a thick lather with the shampoo, covering the entire body and head.

Work it into the coat all the way to the skin. Use a fine shampoo recommended by your veterinarian. Let it stay on the body from 10 to 15 minutes, for this process helps "condition" the skin. If fleas, ticks, or lice are present use a recommended pesticide. Now rinse out the first soaping. Lather a second time and let this lather stay on from 5 to 10 minutes. Now rinse thoroughly, for no soap must remain on the dog. When you do the head, take the muzzle firmly in one hand, tilt the head up and back, and allow the water from the hose or spray to run down the head and neck from a point behind the eyes. Rinse the foreface and chin from underneath.

4. If you think it is necessary and you are not using a recommended shampoo, a creme rinse may be needed. Then after the creme rinse, you should do another complete rinsing.

5. Start the electric dryer so that the Chow accustoms himself to the noise; allow a little time for the dryer to warm up. Set the dryer at "warm", not "hot."

6. Do not dry the dog with towels using a circular motion, which tends to mat and tangle the coat. Instead, use several bath towels for "blotting" the wet coat.

7. Put the Chow on the grooming table—he has by now already shaken off the excess water and has been somewhat "blotted." Begin to brush the dog dry, brushing within the arc of the current of warm air. Hold the dryer about a foot from the dog's coat. *Brush to the skin.* (See section entitled "Grooming the Adult.") If you are still somewhat confused about this method of brushing "to the skin," watch a professional Poodle handler brush his Poodle to the skin, preferably after a bath, if you can arrange to go to the handler's kennel. If not, you can see many professional Poodle handlers brushing their Poodles "to the skin" at local dog shows.

8. When the Chow is absolutely dry—and if you have brushed to the skin—you will be able to use a coarse-tooth comb and run it through the dog's coat several times to make sure no tangles exist. Every hair stands up and glistens beautifully. Every part sparkles and the Chow is the masterpiece of "untouched naturalness" mentioned in the official Chow standard. Even though from tub to show ring may take from three to six or more hours—depending on the Chow's condition before you begin—all the time and effort is worth it. A clean, well-groomed Chow is a more beautiful animal and, one may speculate, a happier, healthier animal.

Ch. Melody's Pandora of Victoria and Ch. Dusten's Kid Shelleen winning Best Brace in Show, Union County Kennel Club 1983. Owned by Cindy Attinello and Dusten Cox, Sharon, Connecticut.

Chapter 12

The Making of a Show Dog

If you have decided to become a show dog exhibitor, you have accepted a very real and very exciting challenge. The groundwork has been accomplished with the selection of your future show prospect. If you have purchased a puppy, we assume that you have gone through all the proper preliminaries concerning good care, which should be the same if the puppy is a pet or future show dog with a few added precautions for the latter.

General Considerations

Remember the importance of keeping your future winner in trim, top condition. Since you want him neither too fat nor too thin, his appetite for his proper diet should be guarded, and children and guests should not be permitted to constantly be feeding him "goodies." The best treat of all is a small wad of raw ground beef or a packaged dog treat. To be avoided are ice cream, cake, cookies, potato chips, and other fattening items which will cause the dog to put on weight and may additionally spoil his appetite for the proper, nourishing, well-balanced diet so essential to good health and condition.

The importance of temperament and showmanship cannot possibly be overestimated. They have put many a mediocre dog across while lack of them can ruin the career of an otherwise outstanding specimen. From the day your dog joins your family, socialize him. Keep him accustomed to being with people and to being handled by people. Encourage your friends and relatives to "go over" him as the judges will in the ring so this will not seem a strange and upsetting experience. Practice showing his "bite" (the manner in which his teeth meet) quickly and deftly. It is quite simple to slip the lips apart with your fingers, and the puppy should be willing to accept this from you or the

Ch. Scotchow Gayla Albert, shown here by breeder Nancy Thompson, is owned by Michael Wolf, Christiana, Pennsylvania. Sired by Ch. Lakeview's Wun Sun of Bro-Ton. Winning the Group at Furniture City in 1981.

This adorable six-months-old puppy is Cassanova's Samson, by Ch. Pandee's Lazarus ex Ch. Pandee's Belle Starr, owner-handled by Kimberly Ann Cunningham. He is here making his first Best of Breed win.

judge without struggle. This is also true of further mouth examination when necessary. Where the standard demands examination of the roof of the mouth and the tongue, accustom the dog to having his jaws opened wide in order for the judge to make this required examination. When missing teeth must be noted, again, teach the dog to permit his jaws to be opened wide and his side lips separated as judges will need to check them one or both of these ways.

Some judges prefer that the exhibitors display the dog's bite and other mouth features themselves. These are the considerate ones, who do not wish to chance the spreading of possible infection from dog to dog with their hands on each one's mouth—a courtesy particularly appreciated in these days of virus epidemics. But the old-fashioned judges still persist in doing it themselves, so the dog should be ready for either possibility.

Take your future show dog with you in the car, thus accustoming him to riding so that he will not become carsick on the day of a dog show. He should associate pleasure and attention with going in the car, or van or motor home. Take him where it is crowded: downtown, to the shops, everywhere you go that dogs are permitted. Make the expeditions fun for him by frequent petting and words of praise; do not just ignore him as you go about your errands.

Do not overly shelter your future show dog. Instinctively you may want to keep him at home where he is safe from germs or danger. This can be foolish on two counts. The first reason is that a puppy kept away from other dogs builds up no natural immunity against all the things with which he will come in contact at dog shows, so it is wiser actually to keep him well up to date on all protective shots and then let him become accustomed to being among dogs and dog owners. Also, a dog who never is among strange people, in strange places, or among strange dogs, may grow up with a shyness or timidity of spirit that will cause you real problems as his show career draws near.

Keep your show prospect's coat in immaculate condition with frequent grooming and daily brushing. When bathing is necessary, use a mild baby shampoo or whatever the breeder of your puppy may suggest. Several of the brand-name products do an excellent job. Be sure to rinse thoroughly so as not to risk skin irritation by traces of soap left behind and protect against soap entering the eyes by a drop of castor oil in each before you lather up. Use warm water (be sure it is not uncomfortably hot or chillingly cold) and a good spray. A hair dryer is a real convenience for the heavily coated breeds and can be used for

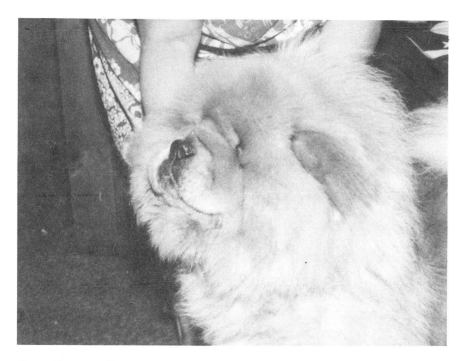

Presenting your Chow's head for the judge's examination. Jeanette of Kamara at one-and-a-half years old. Carl and Marcia Boudreau, owners, Kamara Kennels.

thorough drying after first blotting off the excess moisture with a turkish towel. A wad of cotton in each ear will prevent water entering the ear cavity.

Formation of mats should be watched for carefully in a heavily coated breed, like the Chow Chow, especially behind the ears and underneath the armpits. Toenails also should be watched and trimmed every few weeks. It is important not to permit nails to grow excessively long, as they will ruin the appearance of both the feet and pasterns.

Assuming that you will be handling the dog yourself, or even if he will be professionally handled, a few moments each day of dog show routine is important. Practice setting him up as you have seen the exhibitors do at the shows you've attended, and teach him to hold this position once you have him stacked to your satisfaction. Make the

Note the attentiveness of this beautifully trained show dog as he "baits" for his handler, Jane Forsyth.

Moving a Chow puppy for the judge at a match show. Carl Boudreau owner-handler. The judge is Margaret Ambrose.

learning period pleasant by being firm but lavish in your praise when he responds correctly. Teach him to gait at your side at a moderate rate on a loose lead. When you have mastered the basic essentials at home, then hunt out and join a training class for future work. Training classes are sponsored by show-giving clubs in many areas, and their popularity is steadily increasing. If you have no other way of locating one, perhaps your veterinarian would know of one through some of his other clients; but if you are sufficiently aware of the dog show world to want a show dog, you will probably be personally acquainted with other people who will share information of this type with you.

Accustom your show dog to being in a crate (which you should be doing with a pet dog as well). He should relax in his crate at the shows "between times" for his own well being and safety.

A show dog's teeth must be kept clean and free of tartar. Hard dog-biscuits can help toward this, but if tartar accumulates, see that it is removed promptly by your veterinarian. Bones are not suitable for show dogs as they tend to damage and wear down the tooth enamel.

Match Shows

Your show dog's initial experience in the ring should be in match show competition for several reasons. First, this type of event is intended as a learning experience for both the dog and the exhibitor. You will not feel embarrassed or out of place no matter how poorly your puppy may behave or how inept your attempts at handling may be, as you will find others there with the same type of problems. The important thing is that you get the puppy out and into a show ring where the two of you can practice together and learn the ropes.

Only on rare occasions is it necessary to make match show entries in advance, and even those with a pre-entry policy will usually accept entries at the door as well. Thus you need not plan several weeks ahead, as is the case with point shows, but can go when the mood strikes you. Also there is a vast difference in the cost, as match show entries only cost a few dollars while entry fees for the point shows may be over ten dollars, an amount none of us needs to waste until we have some idea of how the puppy will behave or how much more pre-show training is needed.

Match shows very frequently are judged by professional handlers who, in addition to making the awards, are happy to help new exhibitors with comments and advice on their puppies and their presentation of them. Avail yourself of all these opportunities before heading out to the sophisticated world of the point shows.

Point Shows

As previously mentioned, entries for American Kennel Club point shows must be made in advance. This must be done on an official entry blank of the show-giving club. The entry must then be filed either personally or by mail with the show superintendent or the show secretary (if the event is being run by the club members alone and a superintendent has not been hired, this information will appear on the premium list) in time to reach its destination prior to the published closing date or filling of the quota. These entries must be made carefully, must be signed by the owner of the dog or the owner's agent (your professional handler), and must be accompanied by the entry fee; otherwise they will not be accepted. Remember that it is not when the entry leaves your hands that counts but the date of arrival at its destination. If you are relying on the mails, which are not always dependable, get the entry off well before the deadline to avoid disappointment.

A dog must be entered at a dog show in the name of the actual owner at the time of the entry closing date of that specific show. If a registered dog has been acquired by a new owner, it must be entered in the name of the new owner in any show for which entries close after the date of acquirement, regardless of whether the new owner has or has not actually received the registration certificate indicating that the dog is recorded in his name. State on the entry form whether or not transfer application has been mailed to the American Kennel Club, and it goes without saying that the latter should be attended to promptly when you purchase a registered dog.

In filling out your entry blank, type, print, or write clearly, paying particular attention to the spelling of names, correct registration numbers, and so on.

The Puppy Class is for dogs or bitches who are six months of age and under twelve months, were whelped in the United States, and are not champions. The age of a dog shall be calculated up to and inclusive of the first day of a show. For example, the first day a dog whelped on January 1st is eligible to compete in a Puppy Class at a show is July 1st of the same year; and he may continue to compete in Puppy Classes up to and including a show on December 31st of the same year, but he is *not* eligible to compete in a Puppy Class at a show held on or after January 1st of the following year.

The Puppy Class is the first one in which you should enter your puppy. In it a certain allowance will be made for the fact that they *are* puppies, thus an immature dog or one displaying less than perfect showmanship will be less severely penalized than, for instance, would be the case in Open. It is also quite likely that others in the class will be suffering from these problems, too. When you enter a puppy, be sure to check the classification with care, as some shows divide their Puppy Class into a 6-9 months old section and a 9-12 months old section.

The Novice Class is for dogs six months of age and over, whelped in the United States or Canada, who prior to the official closing date for entries have *not* won three first prizes in the Novice Class, any first prize at all in the Bred-by-Exhibitor, American-bred, or Open Classes, or one or more points toward championship. The provisions for this class are confusing to many people, which is probably the reason exhibitors do not enter in it more frequently. A dog may win any number of first prizes in the Puppy Class and still retain his eligibility for Novice. He may place second, third or fourth not only in Novice on an unlimited number of occasions but also in Bred-by-Exhibitor, American-bred and Open and still remain eligible for Novice. But he may no longer be shown in Novice when he has won three blue ribbons in that class, when he has

Mamie Gregory's famous winner, Ch. Lakeview's Han-Som, handled here by Joe Gregory to Best Non-Sporting Dog at Kennel Club of Philadelphia, December 1967. Mrs. Marie B. Meyer, judge.

won even one blue ribbon in either Bred-by-Exhibitor, American-bred, or Open, or when he has won a single championship point.

In determining whether or not a dog is eligible for the Novice Class, keep in mind the fact that previous wins are calculated according to the official published date for closing of entries, not by the date on which you may actually have made the entry. So if in the interim, between the time you made the entry and the official closing date, your dog makes a win causing him to become ineligible for Novice, change your class *immediately* to another for which he will be eligible, preferably such as either Bred-by-Exhibitor or American-bred. To do this, you must contact the show's superintendent or secretary, at first by telephone to save time and at the same time confirm it in writing. The Novice Class always seems to have the fewest entries of any class, and therefore it is a splendid "practice ground" for you and your young dog while you are getting the "feel" of being in the ring.

Bred-by-Exhibitor Class is for dogs whelped in the United States or, if individually registered in the American Kennel Club Stud Book, for dogs whelped in Canada who are six months of age or older, are not champions, and are owned wholly or in part by the person or by the spouse of the person who was the breeder or one of the breeders of

Ch. Wah Hu's Red cloud Sugar Daddy after winning his first Best in Show his first time out in Mary Vaudo and Zola Coogan's names as a special. Michael Dachel handled on this occasion at Kenilworth Kennel Club, 1982.

record. Dogs entered in this class must be handled in the class by an owner or by a member of the immediate family of the owner. Members of an immediate family for this purpose are husband, wife, father, mother, son, daughter, brother or sister. This is the class which is really the "breeders' showcase," and the one which breeders should enter with particular pride to show off their achievements.

The American-bred Class is for all dogs excepting champions, six months of age or older, who were whelped in the United States by reason of a mating which took place in the United States.

The Open Class is for any dog six months of age or older (this is the only restriction for this class). Dogs with championship points compete in it, dogs who are already champions are eligible to do so, dogs who are imported can be entered, and, of course, American-bred dogs compete in it. This class is, for some strange reason, the favorite of exhibitors who are "out to win." They rush to enter their pointed dogs in it, under the false impression that by doing so they assure themselves of greater attention from the judges. This really is not so, and in my opinion to enter in one of the less competitive classes, with a better chance of winning it and thus earning a second opportunity of gaining

Can. and Bda. Ch. Audrich Dooley O'Toole combines Plainacres and Gotschall's parentage and was bred by Audrey and Richard Meaney, U.S.A. Owned by Marge Ste. Marie, Brossard, P.Q., Canada.

Ch. Ah Sid's the Dilettante, owned by Ah Sid Kennels, handled by Jane Forsyth, taking Best in Show at Ladies Dog Club in 1963.

BEST IN SHOW

Ch. Wah Hu Red Cloud Sugar Daddy, owned by Mary Vaudo and Zola Coogan, Sandwich, Massachusetts, with his handler, William Trainor, after one of his Best in Show wins. When Sugar Daddy ended his show career in July 1984, he had become the Top Winning Chow Chow in breed history.

the judge's approval by returning to the ring in the Winners Class, can often be a more effective strategy.

One does not enter for the Winners Class. One earns the right to compete in it by winning first prize in Puppy, Novice, Bred-by-Exhibitor, American-bred, or Open. No dog who has been defeated on the same day in one of these classes is eligible to compete for Winners, and every dog who has been a blue-ribbon winner in one of them and not defeated in another, should he have been entered in more than one class, (as occasionally happens) *must* do so. Following the selection of the Winners Dog or the Winners Bitch, the dog or bitch receiving that award leaves the ring. Then the dog or bitch who placed second in that class, unless previously beaten by another dog or bitch in another class at the same show, re-enters the ring to compete against the remaining first-prize winners for Reserve. The latter award indicates that the dog or bitch selected for it is standing "in reserve" should the one who received Winners be disqualified or declared ineligible through any technicality when the awards are checked at the American Kennel

Aust. Ch. Hoisan Fuji has been Challenge Bitch at Royal Shows on numerous occasions and Best in Show at two Chow Specialties. Bred and owned by Hoisam Chow Chows, D. and C. Messnarz, Bradbury, New South Wales.

Opposite page: Ch. Wah Hu Red Cloud Sugar Daddy, handled by William Trainor, brings home another Best in Show to Mary Vaudo and Zola Coogan of Sandwich, Massachusetts.

Quasi of Kamara, in the rain and none the worst for it, taking Best of Winners at Windham County Kennel Club, 1983. Owned by Carl and Marcia Boudreau, Kamara Kennels, Rockland, Massachusetts.

Club. In that case, the one who placed Reserve is moved up to Winners, at the same time receiving the appropriate championship points.

Winners Dog and Winners Bitch are the awards which carry points toward championship with them. The points are based on the number of dogs or bitches actually in competition, and the points are scaled one through five, the latter being the greatest number available to any one dog or bitch at any one show. Three-, four-, or five-point wins are considered majors. In order to become a champion, a dog or bitch must have won two majors under two different judges, plus at least one point from a third judge, and the additional points necessary to bring the total to fifteen. When your dog has gained fifteen points as described above, a championship certificate will be issued to you, and your dog's name will be published in the champions of record list in the *Pure-Bred Dogs/American Kennel Gazette,* the official publication of the American Kennel Club.

The scale of championship points for each breed is worked out by the American Kennel Club and reviewed annually, at which time the number required in competition may be either changed (raised or lowered) or remain the same. The scale of championship points for all breeds is published annually in the May issue of the *Gazette,* and the current ratings for each breed within that area are published in every show catalog.

When a dog or bitch is adjudged Best of Winners, its championship points are, for that show, compiled on the basis of which sex had the greater number of points. If there are two points in dogs and four in bitches and the dog goes Best of Winners, then *both* the dog and the bitch are awarded an equal number of points, in this case four. Should the Winners Dog or the Winners Bitch go on to win Best of Breed or Best of Variety, additional points are accorded for the additional dogs and bitches defeated by so doing, provided, of course, that there were entries specifically for Best of Breed Competition or Specials, as these specific entries are generally called.

If your dog or bitch takes Best of Opposite Sex after going Winners, points are credited according to the number of the same sex defeated in both the regular classes and Specials competition. If Best of Winners is also won, then whatever additional points for each of these awards are available will be credited. Many a one- or two-point win has grown into a major in this manner.

Moving further along, should your dog win its Variety Group from the classes (in other words, if it has taken either Winners Dog or Winners Bitch), you then receive points based on the greatest number of points awarded to any member of any breed included within that Group during that show's competition. Should the day's winning also include Best in Show, the same rule of thumb applies, and your dog or bitch receives the highest number of points awarded to any other dog of any breed at that event.

Best of Breed competition consists of the Winners Dog and the Winners Bitch, who automatically compete on the strength of those awards, in addition to whatever dogs and bitches have been entered specifically for this class for which champions of record are eligible. Since July 1980, dogs who, according to their owner's records, have completed the requirements for a championship after the closing of entries for the show, but whose championships are unconfirmed, may be transferred from one of the regular classes to the Best of Breed competition, provided this transfer is made by the show superintendent or show secretary *prior to the start of any judging at the show.*

This has proved an extremely popular new rule, as under it a dog can finish on Saturday and then be transferred and compete as a Special on Sunday. It must be emphasized that the change *must* be made *prior* to the start of *any* part of the day's judging, not for just your individual breed.

In the United States, Best of Breed winners are entitled to compete in the Variety Group which includes them. This is not mandatory, it is a privilege which exhibitors value. (In Canada, Best of Breed winners *must* compete in the Variety Group, or they lose any points already won.) The dogs winning *first* in each of the seven Variety Groups *must* compete for Best in Show. Missing the opportunity of taking your dog in for competition in its Group is foolish as it is there where the general public is most likely to notice your breed and become interested in learning about it.

Non-regular classes are sometimes included at the all-breed shows, and they are almost invariably included at Specialty Shows. These include Stud Dog Class and Brood Bitch Class, which are judged on the basis of the quality of the two offspring accompanying the sire or dam. The quality of the latter two is beside the point and should not be considered by the judge; it is the youngsters who count, and the quality of *both* are to be averaged to decide which sire or dam is the best and most consistent producer. Then there is the Brace Class (which, at all-breed shows, moves up to Best Brace in each Variety Group and then Best Brace in Show), which is judged on the similarity and evenness of

Ch. Cedar Creek's T.G.I. Friday, age eleven months, by Jewell's Supermanchu ex Melody Lane of Cedar Creek was bred by Bonnie Henson and is owned by Barbara Hamon, Oklahoma City, Oklahoma.

Awaiting his turn in the ring, Am., Can., Bda. Ch. Jen-Jen O'Cambellyn at Victoria, B.C. Phyllis Castleton, owner, Anchorage, Alaska.

appearance of the two members of the brace. In other words, the two dogs should look like identical twins in size, color, and conformation and should move together almost as a single dog, one person handling with precision and ease. The same applies to the Team Class competition, except that four dogs are involved and, if necessary, two handlers.

The Veterans Class is for the older dogs, the minimum age of whom is seven years. This class is judged on the quality of the dogs, as the winner competes in Best of Breed competition and has, on a respectable number of occasions, been known to take that top award. So the point is *not* to pick out the oldest dog, as some judges seem to believe, but the best specimen of the breed, exactly as in the regular classes.

224

Ch. Sa-Mi's See My Dolly and Ch. Sa-Mi's El Groucho winning Best Brace of Non Sporting Dogs from judge Bob Wills handled by owner Sarah Parrish.

"Boy and his dog" are well depicted here by Joseph A. Vaudo, Jr. (age nine) and his Mother's famous Chow Chow, Ch. Wah Hu Red Cloud Sugar Daddy, following a Best in Show victory for the latter.

Then there are Sweepstakes and Futurity Stakes sponsored by many Specialty clubs, sometimes as part of their regular Specialty Shows and sometimes as separate events on an entirely different occasion. The difference between the two stakes is that Sweepstakes entries usually include dogs from six to eighteen months age with entries made at the same time as the others for the show while for a Futurity the entries are bitches nominated when bred and the individual puppies entered at or shortly following their birth.

If you already show your dog, if you plan on being an exhibitor in the future, or if you simply enjoy attending dog shows, there is a book, written by me, which you will find to be an invaluable source of detailed information about all aspects of show dog competition. This book is *Successful Dog Show Exhibiting* (T.F.H. Publications, Inc.) and is available wherever the one you are reading was purchased.

Junior Showmanship Competition

If there is a youngster in your family between the ages of ten and sixteen, I can suggest no better or more rewarding hobby than becoming an active participant in Junior Showmanship. This is a marvelous activity for young people. It teaches responsibility, good sportsmanship, the fun of competition where one's own skills are the deciding factor of success, proper care of a pet, and how to socialize with other young folks. Any youngster may experience the thrill of emerging from the ring a winner and the satisfaction of a good job well done.

Entry in Junior Showmanship Classes is open to any boy or girl who is at least ten years old and under seventeen years old on the day of the show. The Novice Junior Showmanship Class is open to youngsters who have not already won, at the time the entries close, three firsts in this class. Youngsters who have won three firsts in Novice may compete in the Open Junior Showmanship Class. Any junior handler who wins his third first-place award in Novice may participate in the Open Class at the same show, provided that the Open Class has at least one other junior handler entered and competing in it that day. The Novice and Open Classes may be divided into Junior and Senior Classes. Youngsters between the ages of ten and twelve, inclusively, are eligible for the Junior division; and youngsters between thirteen and seventeen, inclusively, are eligible for the Senior division.

Any of the foregoing classes may be separated into individual classes for boys and for girls. If such a division is made, it must be so indicated on the premium list. The premium list also indicates the prize for Best Junior Handler, if such a prize is being offered at the show. Any youngster who wins a first in any of the regular classes may enter the competition for this prize, provided the youngster has been undefeated in any other Junior Showmanship Class at that show.

Junior Showmanship Classes, unlike regular conformation classes in which the quality of the dog is judged, are judged solely on the skill and ability of the junior handling the dog. Which dog is best is not the point—it is which youngster does the best job with the dog that is under consideration. Eligibility requirements for the dog being shown in Junior Showmanship, and other detailed information, can be found in *Regulations for Junior Showmanship,* available from the American Kennel Club.

A junior who has a dog that he or she can enter in both Junior Showmanship and conformation classes has twice the opportunity for success and twice the opportunity to get into the ring and work with the dog, a combination which can lead to not only awards for expert handling but also, if the dog is of sufficient quality, for making a conformation champion.

Pre-Show Preparations for Your Dog and You

Preparation of the items you will need as a dog show exhibitor should not be left until the last moment. They should be planned and arranged for at least several days in advance of the show in order for you to remain calm and relaxed as the countdown starts.

The importance of the crate has already been mentioned, and we hope it is already part of your equipment. Of equal importance is the grooming table, which very likely you have also already acquired for use at home. You should take it along with you to the shows, as your dog will need last minute touches before entering the ring. Should you have not yet made this purchase, folding tables with rubber tops are made specifically for this purpose and can be purchased at most dog shows, where concession booths with marvelous assortments of "doggy" necessities are to be found, or at your pet supplier. You will also need a sturdy tack box (also available at the dog show concessions) in which to carry your grooming tools and equipment. The latter should include brushes, comb, scissors, nail clippers, whatever you use for last minute clean-up jobs, cotton swabs, first-aid equipment, and anything you are in the habit of using on the dog, including a leash or two of the type you prefer, some well-cooked and dried-out liver or any of the small packaged "dog treats" for use as bait in the

Ch. Don Lee Chowtime is a noted Best in Show winner, owner handled by Desmond Murphy, under judge Anna Katherine Nicholas.

Ch. Al De Bear Hustler by Ch. Al De Bear Sox Up Starcrest ex Mar Car Mi Soong, was bred by Jan Caruso, is owned by Alan and Deloris Stamm, Jacksonville, Florida.

Ch. Eastward Liontamer of Elster winning the Non-Sporting Group at Westchester Kennel Club 1970, handled by Ted Young, Jr., for Mr. and Mrs. Robert A. Hetherington Jr. and Dr. Samuel Draper.

ring, an atomizer in case you wish to dampen your dog's coat when you are preparing him for the ring, and so on. A large turkish towel to spread under the dog on the grooming table is also useful.

Take a large thermos or cooler of ice, the biggest one you can accommodate in your vehicle, for use by "man and beast." Take a jug of water (there are lightweight, inexpensive ones available at all sporting goods shops) and a water dish. If you plan to feed the dog at the show, or if you and the dog will be away from home more than one day, bring food for him from home so that he will have the type to which he is accustomed.

You may or may not have an exercise pen. Personally I think one a *must*, even if you only have one dog. While the shows do provide areas for the exercise of the dogs, these are among the most likely places to have your dog come in contact with any illnesses which may be going around, and I feel that having a pen of your own for your dog's use is excellent protection. Such a pen can be used in other ways, too, such as a place other than the crate in which to put the dog to relax (that is roomier than the crate) and a place in which the dog can exercise at motels and rest areas. These, too, are available at the show concession stands and come in a variety of heights and sizes. A set of "pooper scoopers" should also be part of your equipment, along with a package of plastic bags for cleaning up after your dog.

Bring along folding chairs for the members of your party, unless all of you are fond of standing, as these are almost never provided anymore by the clubs. Have your name stamped on the chairs so that there will be no doubt as to whom the chairs belong. Bring whatever you and your family enjoy for drinks or snacks in a picnic basket or cooler, as show food, in general, is expensive and usually not great. You should always have a pair of boots, a raincoat, and a rain hat with you (they should remain permanently in your vehicle if you plan to attend shows regularly), as well as a sweater, a warm coat, and a change of shoes. A smock or big cover-up apron will assure that you remain tidy as you prepare the dog for the ring. Your overnight case should include a small sewing kit for emergency repairs, bandaids, headache and indigestion remedies, and any personal products or medications you normally use.

In your car you should always carry maps of the area where you are headed and an assortment of motel directories. Generally speaking, we have found Holiday Inns to be the nicest about taking dogs. Ramadas and Howard Johnsons generally do so cheerfully (with a few excep-

Ch. Dusten's Almond Joy by Ch. Car Mar Pucker for Dusten ex Dusten's Cobbie Cat, moving ahead correctly as a Chow Chow should, handled by John Cox. Dusten and John Cox, owners, Sharon, Connecticut.

tions). Best Western generally frowns on pets (not always, but often enough to make it necessary to find out which do). Some of the smaller chains welcome pets. The majority of privately owned motels do not.

Have everything prepared the night before the show to expedite your departure. Be sure that the dog's identification and your judging program and other show information are in your purse or briefcase. If you are taking sandwiches, have them ready. Anything that goes into the car the night before the show will be one thing less to remember in the morning. Decide upon what you will wear and have it out and ready. If there is any question in your mind about what to wear, try on the possibilities before the day of the show; don't risk feeling you may want to change when you see yourself dressed a few moments prior to departure time!

In planning your outfit, make it something simple that will not detract from your dog. Remember that a dark dog silhouettes attrac-

232

tively against a light background and vice-versa. Sport clothes always seem to look best at dog shows, preferably conservative in type and not overly "loud" as you do not want to detract from your dog, who should be the focus of interest at this point. What you wear on your feet is important. Many types of flooring can be hazardously slippery, as can wet grass. Make it a habit to wear rubber soles and low or flat heels in the ring for your own safety, especially if you are showing a dog that likes to move out smartly.

Your final step in pre-show preparation is to leave yourself plenty of time to reach the show that morning. Traffic can get amazingly heavy as one nears the immediate area of the show, finding a parking place can be difficult, and other delays may occur. You'll be in better humor to enjoy the day if your trip to the show is not fraught with panic over fear of not arriving in time!

AHSO Fan-C Shawnee Cochise, a grandson of Ch. Rhythm's Special Delivery, strikes a super pose on the judging table to win Best of Breed at a 1982 puppy match. Bred by Les and Marilyn Short, Wichita, Kansas.

BEST OF BREED
OR VARIETY
GREATER OCALA
DOG CLUB
APRIL 1982
PHOTO BY Graham

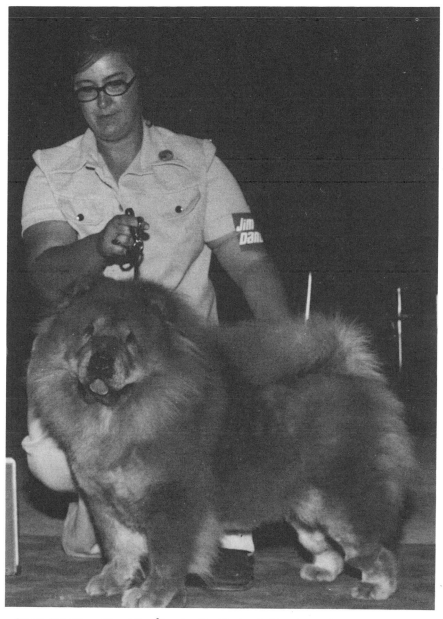

Ch. Sa-Mi's Haun Ting Hing Hua, by Ch. Warlord's Chu-Jen ex Ch. Tsang-Po's Soo Chy, owned by Sarah Parrish, Cantonment, Florida.

Opposite page: Ch. Al De Bear Adonis, cinnamon son of Ch. Heritage Jean Lafitte ex Al De Bear 'Rantin 'N Raven 'N Blue. Breeders-owners, Alan and Deloris Stamm, Jacksonville, Florida.

Westchester 1978. Mrs. Winifred Heckmann is judging Chow Chows here. Desmond J. Murphy at the head of the line with the famous Ch. Don-Lee Chowtime which he co-owns with Susie Donnelly of California.

Enjoying the Dog Show

From the moment of your arrival at the show until after your dog has been judged, keep foremost in your mind the fact the he is your reason for being there and that he should therefore be the center of your attention. Arrive early enough to have time for those last-minute touches that can make such a great difference when he enters the ring. Be sure that he has ample time to exercise and that he attends to personal matters. A dog arriving in the ring and immediately using it as an exercise pen hardly makes a favorable impression on the judge.

When you reach ringside, ask the steward for your arm-card and anchor it firmly into place on your arm. Make sure that you are where you should be when your class is called. The fact that you have picked up your arm-card does not guarantee, as some seem to think, that the judge will wait for you. The judge has a full schedule which he wishes to complete on time. Even though you may be nervous, assume an air of calm self-confidence. Remember that this is a hobby to be enjoyed, so approach it in that state of mind. The dog will do better, too, as he will be quick to reflect your attitude.

Always show your dog with an air of pride. If you make mistakes in presenting him, don't worry about it. Next time you will do better. Do not permit the presence of more experienced exhibitors to intimidate you. After all, they, too, once were newcomers.

The judging routine usually starts when the judge asks that the dogs be gaited in a circle around the ring. During this period the judge is watching each dog as it moves, noting style, topline, reach and drive, head and tail carriage, and general balance. Keep your mind and your eye on your dog, moving him at his most becoming gait and keeping your place in line without coming too close to the exhibitor ahead of you. Always keep your dog on the inside of the circle, between yourself and the judge, so that the judge's view of the dog is unobstructed.

Calmly pose the dog when requested to set up for examination whether on the ground or on a table. If you are at the head of the line and many dogs are in the class, go all the way to the end of the ring before starting to stack the dog, leaving sufficient space for those behind you to line theirs up as well as requested by the judge. If you are not at the head of the line but between other exhibitors, leave sufficient space ahead of your dog for the judge to examine him. The dogs should be spaced so that the judge is able to move among them to see them from all angles. In practicing to "set up" or "stack" your dog for the judge's examination, bear in mind the importance of doing so quickly and with dexterity. The judge has a schedule to meet and only a few moments in which to evaluate each dog. You will immeasurably help yours to make a favorable impression if you are able to "get it all together" in a minimum amount of time. Practice at home before a mirror can be a great help toward bringing this about, facing the dog so that you see him from the same side that the judge will and working to make him look right in the shortest length of time.

Listen carefully as the judge describes the manner in which the dog is to be gaited, whether it is straight down and straight back; down the

Ch. Sa-Mi's Beau Dan Di in 1976 by Te Cu Li's Red Satan ex Lou Bett's Madame Chang Lu. Bred by Elizabeth Smith, owned by Sarah Parrish, Cantonment, Florida.

Opposite page: Mike Larizza (Stonybrook Kennels) winning a Group with the famed Ch. Jen-Sen's China Bear of Palm which he co-owns with Desmond J. Murphy and Mae Palm.

ring, across, and back; or in a triangle. The latter has become the most popular pattern with the majority of judges. "In a triangle" means the dog should move down the outer side of the ring to the first corner, across that end of the ring to the second corner, and then back to the judge from the second corner, using the center of the ring in a diagonal line. Please learn to do this pattern without breaking at each corner to twirl the dog around you, a senseless maneuver we sometimes have noted. Judges like to see the dog in an uninterrupted triangle, as they are thus able to get a better idea of the dog's gait.

It is impossible to overemphasize that the gait at which you move your dog is tremendously important, and considerable study and thought should be given to the matter. At home, have someone move the dog for you at different speeds so that you can tell which shows

Ch. Pandee's Red Sing taking Best in Show at Lancaster Kennel Club, 1961. Imogene P. Earle, owner-handling.

Shenandoah of Kamara at four months, male puppy owned by Michael Leavitt of New Hampshire.

him off to best advantage. The most becoming action almost invariably is seen at a moderate gait, head up and topline holding. Do not gallop your dog around the ring or hurry him into a speed atypical of his breed. Nothing being rushed appears at its best; give your dog a chance to move along at his (and the breed's) natural gait. For a dog's action to be judged accurately, that dog should move with strength and power but not excessive speed, holding a straight line as he goes to and from the judge.

As you bring the dog back to the judge, stop him a few feet away and be sure that he is standing in a becoming position. Bait him to show the judge an alert expression, using whatever tasty morsel he has been trained to expect for this purpose or, if that works better for you, use a small squeak-toy in your hand. A reminder, please, to those using liver or treats. Take them with you when you leave the ring. Do not just drop them on the ground where they will be found by another dog.

When the awards have been made, accept yours graciously, no matter how you actually may feel about it. What's done is done, and arguing with a judge or stomping out of the ring is useless and a reflection on your sportsmanship. Be courteous, congratulate the winner if your dog was defeated, and try not to show your disappointment. By the same token, please be a gracious winner; this, surprisingly, sometimes seems to be still more difficult.

241

Chows enjoy water-sports, too. This is "Charley," bred by Frances Speers and owned by Ruby Pierce.

Chapter 13

Your Dog and Obedience

For its own protection and safety, every dog should be taught, at the very least, to recognize and obey the commands "Come," "Heel," "Down," "Sit," and "Stay." Doing so at some time might save the dog's life and in less extreme circumstances will certainly make him a better behaved, more pleasant member of society. If you are patient and enjoy working with your dog, study some of the excellent books available on the subject of obedience and then teach your canine friend these basic manners. If you need the stimulus of working with a group, find out where obedience training classes are held (usually your veterinarian, your dog's breeder, or a dog-owning friend can tell you) and you and your dog can join up. Alternatively, you could let someone else do the training by sending the dog to class, but this is not very rewarding because you lose the opportunity of working with your dog and the pleasure of the rapport thus established.

If you are going to do it yourself, there are some basic rules which you should follow. You must remain calm and confident in attitude. Never lose your temper and frighten or punish your dog unjustly. Be quick and lavish with praise each time a command is correctly followed. Make it fun for the dog and he will be eager to please you by responding correctly. Repetition is the keynote, but it should not be continued without recess to the point of tedium. Limit the training sessions to ten- or fifteen-minute periods at a time.

Formal obedience training can be followed, and very frequently is, by entering the dog in obedience competition to work toward an obedience degree, or several of them, depending on the dog's aptitude and your own enjoyment. Obedience trials are held in conjunction with the majority of all-breed conformation dog shows, with Specialty shows, and frequently as separate Specialty events. If you are working alone with your dog, a list of trial dates might be obtained from your dog's veterinarian, your dog breeder, or a dog-owning friend; the A.K.C. *Gazette* lists shows and trials to be scheduled in the coming months; and if you are a member of a training class, you will find the information readily available.

The goals for which one works in the formal A.K.C. Member or Licensed Trials are the following titles: Companion Dog (C.D.), Companion Dog Excellent (C.D.X.), and Utility Dog (U.D.). These

Ch. Cabaret Crackerjack, C.D., by Ch. Cabaret Blackjack ex Ch. Cabaret Royal Flush. Bred by Joan and James Richard, owned by Jamie and Joan Richard, Bay City, Michigan. This handsome Chow gained his C.D. title in three consecutive shows.

degrees are earned by receiving three "legs," or qualifying scores, at each level of competition. The degrees must be earned in order, with one completed prior to starting work on the next. For example, a dog must have earned C.D. prior to starting work on C.D.X.; then C.D.X. must be completed before U.D. work begins. The ultimate title attainable in obedience work is Obedience Trial Champion (O.T.Ch.).

When you see the letters "C.D." following a dog's name, you will know that this dog has satisfactorily completed the following exercises: heel on leash, heel free, stand for examination, recall, long sit and long stay. "C.D.X." means that tests have been passed on all of those just mentioned plus heel free, drop on recall, retrieve over high jump, broad jump, long sit, and long down. "U.D." indicates that the dog has additionally passed tests in scent discrimination (leather article), scent discrimination (metal article), signal exercises, directed retrieve, directed jumping, and group stand for examination. The letters "O.T.Ch." are the abbreviation for the only obedience title which precedes rather than follows a dog's name. To gain an obedience trial championship, a dog who already holds a Utility Dog degree must win a total of one hundred points and must win three firsts, under three different judges, in Utility and Open B Classes.

There is also a Tracking Dog title (T.D.) which can be earned at tracking trials. In order to pass the tracking tests the dog must follow the trail of a stranger along a path on which the trail was laid between thirty minutes and two hours previously. Along this track there must be more than two right-angle turns, at least two of which are well out in the open where no fences or other boundaries exist for the guidance of the dog or the handler. The dog wears a harness and is connected to the handler by a lead twenty to forty feet in length. Inconspicuously dropped at the end of the track is an article to be retrieved, usually a glove or wallet, which the dog is expected to locate and the handler to pick up. The letters "T.D.X." are the abbreviation for Tracking Dog Excellent, a more difficult version of the Tracking Dog test with a longer track and more turns to be worked through.

Chapter 14

Breeding Your Chow Chow

The Brood Bitch

We have in an earlier chapter discussed selection of a bitch you plan to use for breeding. In making this important purchase, you will be choosing a bitch who you hope will become the foundation of your kennel. Thus she must be of the finest producing bloodlines, excellent in temperament, of good type, and free of major faults or unsoundness. If you are offered a "bargain" brood bitch, be wary, as for this purchase you should not settle for less than the best and the price will be in accordance with the quality.

Conscientious breeders feel quite strongly that the only possible reason for producing puppies is the ambition to improve and uphold quality and temperament within the breed—definitely *not* because one hopes to make a quick cash profit on a mediocre litter, which never seems to work out that way in the long run and which accomplishes little beyond perhaps adding to the nation's heartbreaking number of unwanted canines. The only reason ever for breeding a litter is, with conscientious people, a desire to improve the quality of dogs in their own kennel or, as pet owners, because they wish to add to the number of dogs they themselves own with a puppy or two from their present favorites. In either case breeding should not take place unless one has definitely prospective owners for as many puppies as the litter may contain, lest you find yourself with several fast-growing young dogs and no homes in which to place them.

Bitches should not be mated earlier than their second season, by which time they should be from fifteen to eighteen months old. Many breeders prefer to wait and first finish the championships of their

Opposite page: Ch. Koby Cassanova of Sweetkins, owned by Mrs. Alan Robson and Mr. Michael Wolf, bred by Steve and Wendy Kobryzycky, handled by Bobby Barlow to Best in Show.

show bitches before breeding them, as pregnancy can be a disaster to a show coat and getting the bitch back in shape again takes time. When you have decided what will be the proper time, start watching at least several months ahead for what you feel would be the perfect mate to best complement your bitch's quality and bloodlines. Subscribe to the magazines which feature your breed exclusively and to some which cover all breeds in order to familiarize yourself with outstanding stud dogs in areas other than your own for there is no necessity nowadays to limit your choice to a nearby dog unless you truly like him and feel that he is the most suitable. It is quite usual to ship a bitch to a stud dog a distance away, and this generally works out with no ill effects. The important thing is that you need a stud dog strong in those features where your bitch is weak or lacking and of bloodlines compatible to hers. Compare the background of both your bitch and the stud dog under consideration, paying particular attention to the quality of the puppies from bitches with backgrounds similar to your bitch's. If the puppies have been of the type and quality you admire, then this dog would seem a sensible choice for yours, too.

Stud fees may be a few hundred dollars, sometimes even more under special situations for a particularly successful sire. It is money well spent, however. Do *not* ever breed to a dog because he is less expensive than the others unless you honestly believe that he can sire the kind of puppies who will be a credit to your kennel and your breed.

Contacting the owners of the stud dogs you find interesting will bring you pedigrees and pictures which you can then study in relation to your bitch's pedigree and conformation. Discuss your plans with other breeders who are knowledgeable (including the one who bred your own bitch). You may not always receive an entirely unbiased opinion (particularly if the person giving it also has an available stud dog), but one learns by discussion so listen to what they say, consider their opinions, and then you may be better qualified to form your own opinion.

As soon as you have made a choice, phone the owner of the stud dog you wish to use to find out if this will be agreeable. You will be asked about the bitch's health, soundness, temperament, and freedom from serious faults. A copy of her pedigree may be requested, as might a picture of her. A discussion of her background over the telephone may be sufficient to assure the stud's owner that she is suitable for the stud dog and of type, breeding, and quality herself to produce puppies of the quality for which the dog is noted. The owner of a top-quality stud is often extremely selective in the bitches permitted to be bred to his dog, in an effort to keep the standard of his puppies high. The owner of a stud dog may require that the bitch be tested for brucellosis, which should be attended to not more than a month previous to the breeding.

Check out which airport will be most convenient for the person meeting and returning the bitch if she is to be shipped and also what airlines use that airport. You will find that the airlines are also apt to have special requirements concerning acceptance of animals for shipping. These include weather limitations and types of crates which are acceptable. The weather limits have to do with extreme heat and extreme cold at the point of destination, as some airlines will not fly dogs into temperatures above or below certain levels, fearing for their safety. The crate problem is a simple one, since if your own crate is not suitable, most of the airlines have specially designed crates available for purchase at a fair and moderate price. It is a good plan to purchase one of these if you intend to be shipping dogs with any sort of frequency. They are made of fiberglass and are the safest type to use for shipping.

Normally you must notify the airline several days in advance to make a reservation, as they are able to accommodate only a certain number of dogs on each flight. Plan on shipping the bitch on about her eighth or ninth day of season, but be careful to avoid shipping her on a weekend, when schedules often vary and freight offices are apt to be closed. Whenever you can, ship your bitch on a direct flight. Changing planes always carries a certain amount of risk of a dog being overlooked or wrongly routed at the middle stop, so avoid this danger if at all possible. The bitch must be accompanied by a health certificate which you must obtain from your veterinarian before taking her to the airport. Usually it will be necessary to have the bitch at the airport about two hours prior to flight time. Before finalizing arrangements, find out from the stud's owner at what time of day it will be most convenient to have the bitch picked up promptly upon arrival.

It is simpler if you can plan to bring the bitch to the stud dog. Some people feel that the trauma of the flight may cause the bitch to not conceive; and, of course, undeniably there is a slight risk in shipping which can be avoided if you are able to drive the bitch to her destination. Be sure to leave yourself sufficient time to assure your arrival at the right time for her for breeding (normally the tenth to fourteenth day following the first signs of color); and remember that if you want the bitch bred twice, you should allow a day to elapse between the two matings. Do not expect the stud's owner to house you while you are there. Locate a nearby motel that takes dogs and make that your headquarters.

Sedna Yung Te, consistently winning young Chow owned by Mrs. C.J. Reed, Guildford, New South Wales, Australia. Littermate to Sedna Chihli Te, owned by Mrs. C.J. Reed, Guildford, new South Wales, Australia.

Just prior to the time your bitch is due in season, you should take her to visit your veterinarian. She should be checked for worms and should receive all the booster shots for which she is due plus one for parvo virus, unless she has had the latter shot fairly recently. The brucellosis test can also be done then, and the health certificate can be obtained for shipping if she is to travel by air. Should the bitch be at all overweight, now is the time to get the surplus off. She should be in good condition, neither underweight nor overweight, at the time of breeding.

The moment you notice the swelling of the vulva, for which you should be checking daily as the time for her season approaches, and the appearance of color, immediately contact the stud's owner and settle on the day for shipping or make the appointment for your arrival with the bitch for breeding. If you are shipping the bitch, the stud fee check should be mailed immediately, leaving ample time for it to have been received when the bitch arrives and the mating takes place. Be sure to call the airline making her reservation at that time, too.

Do not feed the bitch within a few hours before shipping her. Be certain that she has had a drink of water and been well exercised before closing her in the crate. Several layers of newspapers, topped with

Posh Puff at one-and-a-half years old, by Shanghai Southern Tease ex Mai Tai VII, is one of the handsome canine residents at AHSO Fan-C Kennels, Les and Marilyn Short, Wichita, Kansas.

Ch. Ah Sid's The Aide de Kamp adding another win to his record. Dr. Fritz, owner.

some shredded newspaper, make a good bed and can be discarded when she arrives at her destination; these can be replaced with fresh newspapers for her return home. Remember that the bitch should be brought to the airport about two hours before flight time as sometimes the airlines refuse to accept late arrivals.

If you are taking your bitch by car, be certain that you will arrive at a reasonable time of day. Do not appear late in the evening. If your arrival

This is the beautiful Ch. Laral's Excalibur by Weiss, by Ch. Pandee's Dunbar ex Ch. Pandee's Panzarella, one of the most valued stud dogs at Shanghai Kennels, K. Jane Weiss, owner, Pottsville, Pennsylvania.

in town is not until late, get a good night's sleep at your motel and contact the stud's owner first thing in the morning. If possible, leave children and relatives at home, as they will only be in the way and perhaps unwelcome by the stud's owner. Most stud dog owners prefer not to have any unnecessary people on hand during the actual mating.

After the breeding has taken place, if you wish to sit and visit for awhile and the stud's owner has the time, return the bitch to her crate in your car (first ascertaining, of course, that the temperature is comfortable for her and that there is proper ventilation). She should not be permitted to urinate for at least one hour following the breeding. This is the time when you get the business part of the transaction attended to. Pay the stud fee, upon which you should receive your breeding certificate and, if you do not already have it, a copy of the stud dog's pedigree. The owner of the stud dog does not sign or furnish a litter registration application until the puppies have been born.

Upon your return home, you can settle down and plan in happy anticipation a wonderful litter of puppies. A word of caution! Remember that although she has been bred, your bitch is still an interesting target for all male dogs, so guard her carefully for the next week or until you are absolutely certain that her season has entirely ended. This would be no time to have any unfortunate incident with another dog.

The Stud Dog

Choosing the best stud dog to complement your bitch is often very difficult. The two principal factors to be considered should be the stud's conformation and his pedigree. Conformation is fairly obvious; you want a dog that is typical of the breed in the words of the standard of perfection. Understanding pedigrees is a bit more subtle since the pedigree lists the ancestry of the dog and involves individuals and bloodlines with which you may not be entirely familiar.

To a novice in the breed, then, the correct interpretation of a pedigree may at first be difficult to grasp. Study the pictures and text of this book and you will find many names of important bloodlines and members of the breed. Also make an effort to discuss the various dogs behind the proposed stud with some of the more experienced breeders, starting with the breeder of your own bitch. Frequently these folks will be personally familiar with many of the dogs in question, can offer opinions of them, and may have access to additional pictures which you would benefit by seeing.

Am., Can., Bda. Ch. Jen Jen O'Cambellyn, handled by Renee Marcy was the Number 1 Non-Sporting Dog in Alaska for 1981 and Number 2 for 1982. He has been out of the Group only one time since his arrival in Alaska in 1980. Phyllis Castleton, owner, Anchorage, Alaska.

Opposite page: Ch. Fa-Ci Willow here is owner-handled by Michael Wolf to Best of Breed at Westminster in 1976.

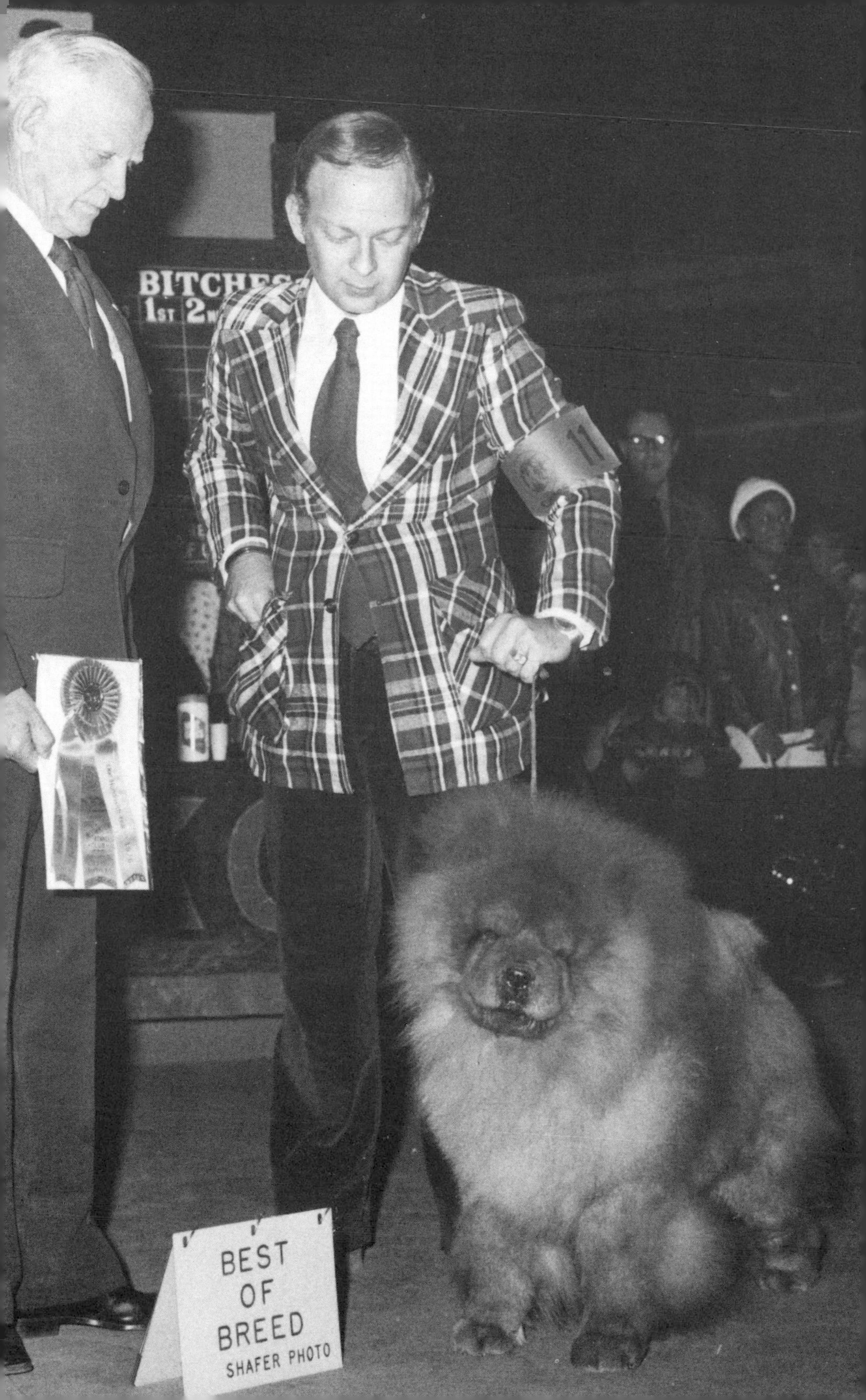
BITCHES
1ST 2N
BEST OF BREED
SHAFER PHOTO

Ponca City Kennel Club Match. *Left to right,* AHSO Fan-C Comanche Warbonnet; future Ch. Shanghai Mastradomas of AHSO; and AHSO Fan-C Ruffles 'n Flourishes. Three promising puppies gaining match show experience prior to entering the big time! AHSO Fan-C Chows, Les and Marilyn Short, Wichita, Kansas.

It is very important that the stud's pedigree should be harmonious with that of the bitch you plan on breeding to him. Do not rush out and breed to the latest winner with no thought of whether or not he can produce true quality. By no means are all great show dogs great producers. It is the producing record of the dog in question and the dogs and bitches from which he has come which should be the basis on which you make your choice.

Breeding dogs is never a money-making operation. By the time you pay a stud fee, care for the bitch during pregnancy, whelp the litter, and rear the puppies through their early shots, worming, and so on, you will be fortunate to break even financially once the puppies have been sold. Your chances of doing this are greater if you are breeding for a show-quality litter which will bring you higher prices as the pups are sold as show prospects. Therefore; your wisest investment is to use the best dog available for your bitch regardless of the cost; then you should wind up with more valuable puppies. Remember that it is equally costly to raise mediocre puppies as top ones, and your chances of financial return are better on the latter. To breed to the most excellent, most suitable stud dog you can find is the only sensible thing to do, and it is poor economy to quibble over the amount you are paying in stud fee.

It will be your decision which course you decide to follow when you breed your bitch, as there are three options: line-breeding, inbreeding,

Ch. Pinewoods Hickory Dic, "Comanche," on the way to his title at Wichita Kennel Club his first time in the ring. Handled by owner, Les Short, AHSO Fan-C Chows, Wichita, Kansas.

and outcrossing. Each of these methods has its supporters and its detractors! Line-breeding is breeding a bitch to a dog belonging originally to the same canine family, being descended from the same ancestors, such as half-brother to half-sister, grandsire to granddaughters, niece to uncle (and vice-versa) or cousin to cousin. Inbreeding is breeding father to daughter, mother to son, or full brother to sister. Outcross breeding is breeding a dog and a bitch with no or only a few mutual ancestors.

Line-breeding is probably the safest course, and the one most likely to bring results, for the novice breeder. The more sophisticated inbreeding should be left to the experienced, long-time breeders who thoroughly know and understand the risks and the possibilities involved with a particular line. It is usually done in an effort to intensify some ideal feature in that strain. Outcrossing is the reverse of inbreeding, an effort to introduce improvement in a specific feature needing correction, such as a shorter back, better movement, more correct head or coat, and so on.

It is the serious breeder's ambition to develop a strain or bloodline of their own, one strong in qualities for which their dogs will become distinguished. However, it must be realized that this will involve time, patience, and at least several generations before the achievement can be claimed. The safest way to embark on this plan, as we have mentioned, is by the selection and breeding of one or two bitches, the best you can buy and from top-producing kennels. In the beginning you do *not* really have to own a stud dog. In the long run it is less expensive and sounder judgment to pay a stud fee when you are ready to breed a bitch than to purchase a stud dog and feed him all year; a stud dog does not win any popularity contests with owners of bitches to be bred until he becomes a champion, has been successfully Specialed for awhile, and has been at least moderately advertised, all of which adds up to a quite healthy expenditure.

The wisest course for the inexperienced breeder just starting out in dogs is as I have outlined above. Keep the best bitch puppy from the first several litters. After that you may wish to consider keeping your own stud dog if there has been a particularly handsome male in one of your litters that you feel has great potential or if you know where there is one available that you are interested in, with the feeling that he would work in nicely with the breeding program on which you have embarked. By this time, with several litters already born, your eye should have developed to a point enabling you to make a wise choice, either from one of your own litters or from among dogs you have seen that appear suitable.

The greatest care should be taken in the selection of your own stud dog. He must be of true type and highest quality as he may be responsible for siring many puppies each year, and he should come from a line of excellent dogs on both sides of his pedigree which themselves are, and which are descended from, successful producers. This dog should have no glaring faults in conformation; he should be of such quality that he can hold his own in keenest competition within his breed. He should be in good health, be virile and be a keen stud dog, a proven sire able to transmit his correct qualities to his puppies. Need I say that such a dog will be enormously expensive unless you have the good fortune to produce him in one of your own litters? To buy and use a lesser stud dog, however, is downgrading your breeding program unnecessarily since there are so many dogs fitting the description of a fine stud whose services can be used on payment of a stud fee.

You should *never* breed to an unsound dog or one with any serious standard or disqualifying faults. Not all champions by any means pass along their best features; and by the same token, occasionally you will find a great one who can pass along his best features but never gained his championship title due to some unusual circumstances. The information you need about a stud dog is what type of puppies he has produced and with what bloodlines and whether or not he possesses the bloodlines and attributes considered characteristic of the best in your breed.

If you go out to buy a stud dog, obviously he will not be a puppy but rather a fully mature and proven male with as many of the best attributes as possible. True, he will be an expensive investment, but if you choose and make his selection with care and forethought, he may well prove to be one of the best investments you have ever made.

Of course, the most exciting of all is when a young male you have decided to keep from one of your litters due to his tremendous show potential turns out to be a stud dog such as we have described. In this case he should be managed with care, for he is a valuable property that can contribute inestimably to his breed as a whole and to your own kennel specifically.

Do not permit your stud dog to be used until he is about a year old, and even then he should be bred to a mature, proven matron accustomed to breeding who will make his first experience pleasant and easy. A young dog can be put off forever by a maiden bitch who fights and resists his advances. Never allow this to happen. Always start a stud dog out with a bitch who is mature, has been bred previously, and is of even temperament. The first breeding should be performed in quiet surroundings with only you and one other person to hold the bitch. Do not make it a circus, as the experience will determine the dog's outlook about future stud work. If he does not enjoy the first experience or associates it with any unpleasantness, you may well have a problem in the future.

Your young stud must permit help with the breeding, as later there will be bitches who will not be cooperative. If right from the beginning you are there helping him and praising him whether or not your assistance is actually needed, he will expect and accept this as a matter of course when a difficult bitch comes along.

Things to have handy before introducing your dog and the bitch are K-Y jelly (the only lubricant which should be used) and a length of gauze with which to muzzle the bitch should it be necessary to keep her from biting you or the dog. Some bitches put up a fight; others are calm. It is best to be prepared.

Sedna The Genesis relaxes at home. Mrs. C.J. Reed, owner, Sedna Chow Chows, Guildford, New South Wales.

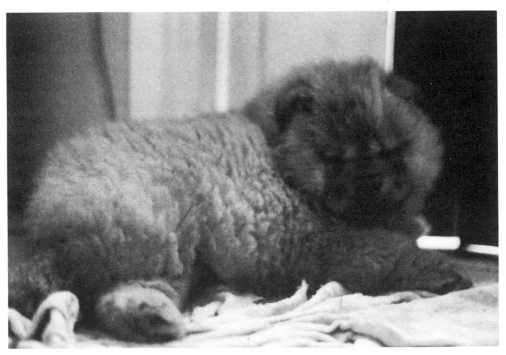

Nine-year-old Ashley Hampton having a very happy day with her three-months-old puppy, first time in the ring, as she wins Best in Match at Vicksburg, Virginia. Bred by Les and Marilyn Short, owned by Anne and Ashley Hampton, this baby is by Ch. Pinewood's Hickory Dic ex AHSO Topaz Trophy, and is named AHSO Comanche War Drummer AHSHI.

At the time of the breeding the stud fee comes due, and it is expected that it will be paid promptly. Normally a return service is offered in case the bitch misses or fails to produce one live puppy. Conditions of the service are what the stud dog's owner makes them, and there are no standard rules covering this. The stud fee is paid for the act, not the result. If the bitch fails to conceive, it is customary for the owner to offer a free return service; but this is a courtesy and not to be considered a right, particularly in the case of a proven stud who is siring consistently and whose fault the failure obviously is *not*. Stud dog owners are always anxious to see their clients get good value and to have in the ring winning young stock by their dog; therefore, very few refuse to mate the second time. It is wise, however, for both parties to have the terms of the transaction clearly understood at the time of the breeding.

If the return service has been provided and the bitch has missed a second time, that is considered to be the end of the matter and the owner would be expected to pay a further fee if it is felt that the bitch should be given a third chance with the stud dog. The management of a stud dog and his visiting bitches is quite a task, and a stud fee has usually been well earned when one service has been achieved, let alone by repeated visits from the same bitch.

The accepted litter is one live puppy. It is wise to have printed a breeding certificate which the owner of the stud dog and the owner of the bitch both sign. This should list in detail the conditions of the breeding as well as the dates of the mating.

Upon occasion, arrangements other than a stud fee in cash are made for a breeding, such as the owner of the stud taking a pick-of-the-litter puppy in lieu of money. This should be clearly specified on the breeding certificate along with the terms of the age at which the stud's owner will select the puppy, whether it is to be a specific sex, or whether it is to be the pick of the entire litter.

The price of a stud fee varies according to circumstances. Usually, to prove a young stud dog, his owner will allow the first breeding to be quite inexpensive. Then, once a bitch has become pregnant by him, he becomes a "proven stud" and the fee rises accordingly for bitches that follow. The sire of championship-quality puppies will bring a stud fee of at least the purchase price of one show puppy as the accepted "rule-of-thumb." Until at least one champion by your stud dog has finished,

Mrs. C.J. Reed's granddaughter, Rebecca, with Sedna Fortune Cookie, by Tsulin Bhuda ex Sedna Shandy Kid. Sedna Kennels, Guildford, New South Wales.

Cedar Creek Chow puppies. Frances Speers, owner, Oklahoma City, Oklahoma.

the fee will remain equal to the price of one pet puppy. When his list of champions starts to grow, so does the amount of the stud fee. For a top-producing sire of champions, the stud fee will rise accordingly.

Almost invariably it is the bitch who comes to the stud dog for the breeding. Immediately upon having selected the stud dog you wish to use, discuss the possibility with the owner of that dog. It is the stud dog owner's prerogative to refuse to breed any bitch deemed unsuitable for his dog. Stud fee and method of payment should be stated at this time, and a decision reached on whether it is to be a full cash transaction at the time of the mating or a pick-of-the-litter puppy, usually at eight weeks of age.

If the owner of the stud dog must travel to an airport to meet the bitch and ship her for the flight home, an additional charge will be made for time, tolls, and gasoline based on the stud owner's proximity to the airport. The stud fee includes board for the day on the bitch's arrival through two days for breeding, with a day in between. If it is necessary that the bitch remain longer, it is very likely that additional board will be charged at the normal per-day rate for the breed.

Be sure to advise the stud's owner as soon as you know that your bitch is in season so that the stud dog will be available. This is

263

especially important because if he is a dog being shown, he and his owner may be unavailable owing to the dog's absence from home.

As the owner of a stud dog being offered to the public, it is essential that you have proper facilities for the care of visiting bitches. Nothing can be worse than a bitch being insecurely housed and slipping out to become lost or bred by the wrong dog. If you are taking people's valued bitches into your kennel or home, it is imperative that you provide them with comfortable, secure housing and good care while they are your responsibility.

There is no dog more valuable than the proven sire of champions, Group winners, and Best in Show dogs. Once you have such an animal, guard his reputation well and do *not* permit him to be bred to just any bitch that comes along. It takes two to make the puppies; even the most dominant stud can not do it all himself, so never permit him to breed a bitch you consider unworthy. Remember that when the puppies arrive, it will be your stud dog who will be blamed for any lack of quality, while the bitch's shortcomings will be quickly and conveniently overlooked.

Going into the actual management of the mating is a bit superfluous here. If you have had previous experience in breeding a dog and bitch you will know how the mating is done. If you do not have such experience, you should not attempt to follow directions given in a book but should have a veterinarian, breeder friend, or handler there to help you the first few times. You do not just turn the dog and bitch loose together and await developments, as too many things can go wrong and you may altogether miss getting the bitch bred. Someone should hold the dog and the bitch (one person each) until the "tie" is made and these two people should stay with them during the entire act.

If you get a complete tie, probably only the one mating is absolutely necessary. However, especially with a maiden bitch or one that has come a long distance for this breeding, we prefer following up with a second breeding, leaving one day in between the two matings. In this way there will be little or no chance of the bitch missing.

Once the tie has been completed and the dogs release, be certain that the male's penis goes completely back within its sheath. He should be allowed a drink of water and a short walk, and then he should be put into his crate or somewhere alone where he can settle down. Do not allow him to be with other dogs for a while as they will notice the odor of the bitch on him, and particularly with other males present, he may become involved in a fight.

Pregnancy, Whelping, and the Litter

Once the bitch has been bred and is back at home, remember to keep an ever watchful eye that no other male gets to her until at least the twenty-second day of her season has passed. Until then, it will still be possible for an unwanted breeding to take place, which at this point would be catastrophic. Remember that she actually can have two separate litters by two different dogs, so take care.

In other ways, she should be treated normally. Controlled exercise is good, and necessary for the bitch throughout her pregnancy, tapering it off to just several short walks daily, preferably on lead, as she reaches about her seventh week. As her time grows close, be careful about her jumping or playing too roughly.

The theory that a bitch should be overstuffed with food when pregnant is a poor one. A fat bitch is never an easy whelper, so the overfeeding you consider good for her may well turn out to be the exact opposite. During the first few weeks of pregnancy, your bitch should be fed her normal diet. At four to five weeks along, calcium should be added to her food. At seven weeks her food may be increased if she seems to crave more than she is getting, and a meal of canned milk (mixed with an equal amount of water) should be introduced. If she is fed just once a day, add another meal rather than overload her with too much at one time. If twice a day is her schedule, then a bit more food can be added to each feeding.

A week before the pups are due, your bitch should be introduced to her whelping box so that she will be accustomed to it and feel at home there when the puppies arrive. She should be encouraged to sleep there but permitted to come and go as she wishes. The box should be roomy enough for her to lie down and stretch out but not too large lest the pups have more room than is needed in which to roam and possibly get chilled by going too far away from their mother. Be sure that the box has a "pig rail"; this will prevent the puppies from being crushed against the sides. The room in which the box is placed, either in your home or in the kennel, should be kept at about 70 degrees Fahrenheit. In winter it may be necessary to have an infrared lamp over the whelping box, in which case be careful not to place it too low or close to the puppies.

Newspapers will become a very important commodity, so start collecting them well in advance to have a big pile handy to the whelping box. With a litter of puppies, one never seems to have papers enough, so the higher pile to start with, the better off you will be. Other necessities for whelping time are clean, soft turkish towels, scissors, and a bottle of alcohol.

You will know that her time is very near when your bitch becomes restless, wandering in and out of her box and of the room. She may refuse food, and at that point her temperature will start to drop. She will dig at and tear up the newspapers in her box, shiver, and generally look uncomfortable. Only you should be with your bitch at this time. She does not need spectators; and several people, even though they may be family members whom she knows, hanging over her may upset her to the point where she may harm the puppies. You should remain nearby, quietly watching, not fussing or hovering; speak calmly and frequently to her to instill confidence. Eventually she will settle down in her box and begin panting; contractions will follow. Soon thereafter a puppy will start to emerge, sliding out with the contractions. The mother immediately should open the sac, sever the cord with her teeth, and then clean up the puppy. She will also eat the placenta, which you should permit. Once the puppy is cleaned, it should be placed next to the bitch unless she is showing signs of having the next one immediately. Almost at once the puppy will start looking for a nipple on which to nurse, and you should ascertain that it is able to latch on successfully.

If the puppy is a breech (*i.e.,* born feet first), you must watch carefully for it to be completely delivered as quickly as possible and the sac removed quickly so that the puppy does not drown. Sometimes even a normally positioned birth will seem extremely slow in coming. Should this occur, you might take a clean towel and, as the bitch contracts, pull the puppy out, doing so gently and with utmost care. If, once the puppy is delivered, it shows little signs of life, take a rough turkish towel and massage the puppy's chest by rubbing quite briskly back and forth. Continue this for about fifteen minutes, and be sure that the mouth is free from liquid. It may be necessary to try mouth-to-mouth breathing, which is done by pressing the puppy's jaws open and, using a finger, depressing the tongue which may be stuck to the roof of the mouth. Then place your mouth against the puppy's and blow hard down the puppy's throat. Bubbles may pop out of its nose, but keep on blowing. Rub the puppy's chest with the towel again and try artificial respiration, pressing the sides of the chest together slowly and rhythmically—in and out, in and out. Keep trying one method or the other for at least twenty minutes before giving up. You may be rewarded with a live puppy who otherwise would not have made it.

Thea Reimers caught these poses of her lovely Chow Chow, Sunswept Bounty of T' Bae-Rey (Ch. Sunswept Tonk's Full Tank ex Ch. Sunswept Saucity) enjoying the holiday season. Bred by Mrs. Barbara Durst.

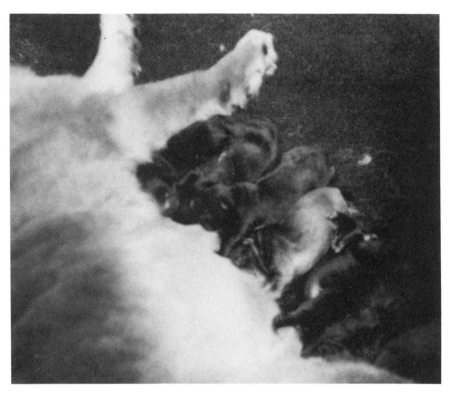

These seven three-day-old Sunswept puppies are enjoying dinner time at
Sunswept Kennels, Barbara Durst, Parkton, Maryland.

If you are successful in bringing the puppy around, do not immediately put it back with the mother as it should be kept extra warm.
Put it in a cardboard box on an electric heating pad or, if it is the time
of year when your heat is running, near a radiator or near the fireplace
or stove. As soon as the rest of the litter has been born it then can join
the others.

An hour or more may elapse between puppies, which is fine so long
as the bitch seems comfortable and is neither straining nor contract-
ing. She should not be permitted to remain unassisted for more than
an hour if she does continue to contract. This is when you should get
her to your veterinarian, whom you should already have alerted to the
possibility of a problem existing. He should examine her and perhaps
give her a shot of Pituitrin. In some cases the veterinarian may find
that a Caesarean section is necessary due to a puppy being lodged in a
manner making normal delivery impossible. Sometimes this is caused

by an abnormally large puppy, or it may just be that the puppy is simply turned in the wrong position. If the bitch does require a Caesarean section, the puppies already born must be kept warm in their cardboard box with a heating pad under the box.

Once the section is done, get the bitch and the puppies home. Do not attempt to put the puppies in with the bitch until she has regained consciousness as she may unknowingly hurt them. But do get them back to her as soon as possible for them to start nursing.

Should the mother lack milk at this time, the puppies must be fed by hand, kept very warm, and held onto the mother's teats several times a day in order to stimulate and encourage the secretion of milk, which should start shortly.

Assuming that there has been no problem and that the bitch has whelped naturally, you should insist that she go out to exercise, staying just long enough to make herself comfortable. She can be offered a bowl

Misty de Guiberdy surrounded by her babies. Mr. and Mrs. Maurice Lacroix, owners, Bromont, P.Q., Canada.

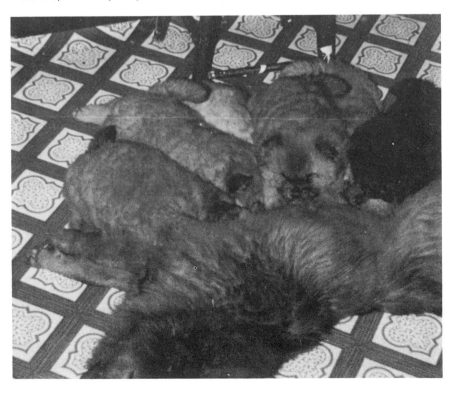

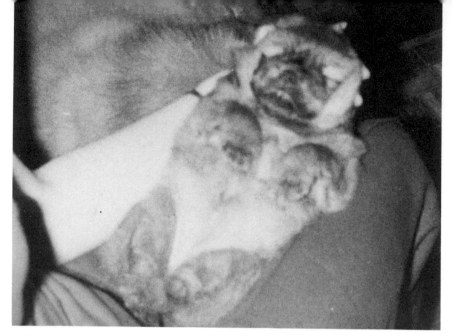

Misty's first female puppy. Mr. and Mrs. Maurice Lacroix, Bromont, Quebec, Canada.

of milk and a biscuit, but then she should settle down with her family. Freshen the whelping box for her with fresh newspapers while she is taking this respite so that she and the puppies will have a clean bed.

Unless some problem arises, there is little you must do about the puppies until they become three to four weeks old. Keep the box clean and supplied with fresh newspapers the first few days, but then turkish towels should be tacked down to the bottom of the box so that the puppies will have traction as they move about.

If the bitch has difficulties with her milk supply, or if you should be so unfortunate as to lose her, then you must be prepared to either hand-feed or tube-feed the puppies if they are to survive. We personally prefer tube-feeding as it is so much faster and easier. If the bitch is available, it is best that she continues to clean and care for the puppies in the normal manner excepting for the food supplements you will provide. If it is impossible for her to do this, then after every feeding you must gently rub each puppy's abdomen with wet cotton to make it urinate, and the rectum should be gently rubbed to open the bowels.

Newborn puppies must be fed every three to four hours around the clock. The puppies must be kept warm during this time. Have your veterinarian teach you how to tube-feed. You will find that it is really quite simple.

After a normal whelping, the bitch will require additional food to enable her to produce sufficient milk. In addition to being fed twice daily, she should be given some canned milk several times each day.

When the puppies are two weeks old, their nails should be clipped, as they are needle sharp at this age and can hurt or damage the mother's teats and stomach as the pups hold on to nurse.

Between three and four weeks of age, the puppies should begin to be weaned. Scraped beef (prepared by scraping it off slices of beef with a spoon so that none of the gristle is included) may be offered in very small quantities a couple of times daily for the first few days. Then by the third day you can mix puppy chow with warm water as directed on the package, offering it four times daily. By now the mother should be kept away from the puppies and out of the box for several hours at a time so that when they have reached five weeks of age she is left in with them only overnight. By the time the puppies are six weeks old, they should be entirely weaned and receiving only occasional visits from their mother.

Most veterinarians recommend a temporary DHL (distemper, hepatitis, leptospirosis) shot when the puppies are six weeks of age. This remains effective for about two weeks. Then at eight weeks of age, the puppies should receive the series of permanent shots for DHL protection. It is also a good idea to discuss with your vet the advisability of having your puppies inoculated against the dreaded parvovirus at the same time. Each time the pups go to the vet for shots, you should bring stool samples so that they can be examined for worms. Worms go through various stages of development and may be present in a stool sample even though the sample does not test positive in every checkup. So do not neglect to keep careful watch on this.

The puppies should be fed four times daily until they are three months old. Then you can cut back to three feedings daily. By the time the puppies are six months of age, two meals daily are sufficient. Some people feed their dogs twice daily throughout their lifetime; others go to one meal daily when the puppy becomes one year of age.

The ideal age for puppies to go to their new homes is between eight and twelve weeks, although some puppies successfully adjust to a new home when they are six weeks old. Be sure that they go to their new owners accompanied by a description of the diet you've been feeding them and a schedule of the shots they have already received and those they still need. These should be included with the registration application and a copy of the pedigree.

On the sign:
URGIS
EL CLUB
ST 19 1976
N ON
ORTING
ROUP

U D G E
RK THOMPSON

BOOTH
PHOTO

NON SPORTING GROUP

At only eleven months of age, future Best in Show dog Ch. Cabaret Joker already showing the potential he so beautifully fulfilled, winning the Non-Sporting Group from the Bred-by Exhibitor Class under Clark Thompson. Here, handled by Joan Richard who bred and co-owns him, Cabaret Chows, Bay City, Michigan.

Chapter 15

Traveling with Your Dog

When you travel with your dog, to shows or on vacation or wherever, remember that everyone does not share our enthusiasm or love for dogs and that those who do not, strange creatures though they seem to us, have their rights, too. These rights, on which we should not encroach, include not being disturbed, annoyed, or made uncomfortable by the presence and behavior of other people's pets. Your dog should be kept on lead in public places and should recognize and promptly obey the commands "Down," "Come," "Sit," and "Stay."

Take along his crate if you are going any distance with your dog. And keep him in it when riding in the car. A crated dog has a far better chance of escaping injury than one riding loose in the car should an accident occur or an emergency arise. If you do permit your dog to ride loose, never allow him to hang out a window, ears blowing in the breeze. An injury to his eyes could occur in this manner. He could also become overly excited by something he sees and jump out, or he could lose his balance and fall out.

Never, ever under any circumstances, should a dog be permitted to ride loose in the back of a pick-up truck. I have noted, with horror, that some people do transport dogs in this manner, and I think it cruel and shocking. How easily such a dog can be thrown out of the truck by sudden jolts or an impact! And I am sure that many dogs have jumped out at the sight of something exciting along the way. Some unthinking individuals tie the dog, probably not realizing that were he to jump under those circumstances, his neck would be broken, he could be dragged alongside the vehicle, or he could be hit by another vehicle. If you are for any reason taking your dog in an open back truck, please have sufficient regard for that dog to at least provide a crate for him, and then remember that, in or out of a crate, a dog riding under the

A group-placer from the 6-9 months puppy class, Sa-Mi's Go Stick It is by Ch. Sa-Mi That Away To Mara ex Ch. Sa-Mi's Go Stuff It and was bred and is owned by Sarah Parrish, Sa-Mi Chow Chows.

direct rays of the sun in hot weather can suffer and have his life endangered by the heat.

If you are staying at a hotel or motel with your dog, exercise him somewhere other than in the flower beds and parking lot of the property. People walking to and from their cars really are not thrilled at "stepping in something" left by your dog. Should an accident occur, pick it up with a tissue or a paper towel and deposit it in a proper receptacle; do not just walk off leaving it to remain there. Usually there are grassy areas on the sides of and behind motels where dogs can be exercised. Use them rather than the more conspicuous, usually carefully tended, front areas or those close to the rooms. If you are becoming a dog show enthusiast, you will eventually need an exercise pen to take with you to the show. Exercise pens are ideal to use when staying at motels, too, as they permit you to limit the dog's roaming space and to pick up after him more easily.

Never leave your dog unattended in the room of a motel unless you are absolutely, positively certain that he will stay there quietly and not damage or destroy anything. You do not want a long list of complaints from irate guests, caused by the annoying barking or whining of a lonesome dog in strange surroundings or an overzealous watch dog barking furiously each time a footstep passes the door or he hears a sound from an adjoining room. And you certainly do not want to return to torn curtains or bedspreads, soiled rugs, or other embarrassing evidence of the fact that your dog is not really house-reliable after all.

If yours is a dog accustomed to traveling with you and you are positive that his behavior will be acceptable when left alone, that is fine. But if the slightest uncertainty exists, the wise course is to leave him in the car while you go to dinner or elsewhere; then bring him into the room when you are ready to retire for the night.

When you travel with a dog, it is often simpler to take along from home the food and water he will need rather than buying food and looking for water while you travel. In this way he will have the rations to which he is accustomed and which you know agree with him, and there will be no fear of problems due to different drinking water. Feeding on the road is quite easy now, at least for short trips, with all the splendid dry prepared foods and high-quality canned meats available. A variety of lightweight, refillable water containers can be bought at many types of stores.

If you are going to another country, you will need a health certificate from your veterinarian for each dog you are taking with you, certifying that each has had rabies shots within the required time preceding your visit.

Be careful always to leave sufficient openings to ventilate your car when the dog will be alone in it. Remember that during the summer, the rays of the sun can make an inferno of a closed car within only a few minutes, so leave enough window space open to provide air circulation. Again, if your dog is in a crate, this can be done quite safely. The fact that you have left the car in a shady spot is not always a guarantee that you will find conditions the same when you return. Don't forget that the position of the sun changes in a matter of minutes, and the car you left nicely shaded half an hour ago can be getting full sunlight far more quickly than you may realize. So, if you leave a dog in the car, make sure there is sufficient ventilation and check back frequently to ascertain that all is well.

Ah Sid Belle Star, by Ch. Pandee Silver Mug ex Chang Shi Honey, bred by Joan Wellborn of Ah Sid Kennels, was one of the early Chows at Dusten's. Belle lived to the ripe old age of sixteen years one month, and was ten years old in this photo. Dusten and John Cox, owners, Sharon, Connecticut.

Chapter 15

Responsibilities of
Breeders and Owners

The first responsibility of any person breeding dogs is to do so with care, forethought, and deliberation. It is inexcusable to breed more litters than you need to carry on your show program or to perpetuate your bloodlines. A responsible breeder should not cause a litter to be born without definite plans for the safe and happy disposition of the puppies.

A responsible dog breeder makes absolutely certain, so far as is humanly possible, that the home to which one of his puppies will go is a good home, one that offers proper care and an enthusiastic owner. I have tremendous admiration for those people who insist on visiting (although doing so is not always feasible) the prospective owners of their puppies, to see if they have suitable facilities for keeping a dog, that they understand the responsibility involved, and that all members of the household are in accord regarding the desirability of owning one. All breeders should carefully check out the credentials of prospective purchasers to be sure that the puppy is being placed in responsible hands.

I am certain that no breeder ever wants a puppy or grown dog he has raised to wind up in an animal shelter, in an experimental laboratory, or as a victim of a speeding car. While complete control of such a situation may be impossible, it is at least our responsibility to make every effort to turn over dogs to responsible people. When selling a puppy, it is a good idea to do so with the understanding that should it become necessary to place the dog in other hands, the purchaser will first contact you, the breeder. You may want to help in some way, possibly by buying or taking back the dog or placing it elsewhere. It is not fair just to sell our puppies and then never again give a thought to their welfare. Family problems arise, people may be forced to move where dogs are prohibited, or people just plain grow bored with a dog and its care. Thus the dog becomes a victim. You, as the dog's breeder, should concern yourself with the welfare of each of your dogs and see to it that the dog remains in good hands.

The final obligation every dog owner shares, be there just one dog or an entire kennel involved, is that of making detailed, explicit plans for the future of our dearly loved animals in the event of the owner's death. Far too many of us are apt to procrastinate and leave this very important matter unattended to, feeling that everything will work out or that "someone will see to them." The latter is not too likely, at least not to the benefit of the dogs, unless you have done some advance planning which will assure their future well-being.

Life is filled with the unexpected, and even the youngest, healthiest, most robust of us may be the victim of a fatal accident or sudden illness. The fate of our dogs, so entirely in our hands, should never be left to chance. If you have not already done so, please get together with your lawyer and set up a clause in your will specifying what you want done with each of your dogs, to whom they will be entrusted (after first making absolutely certain that the person selected is willing and able to assume the responsibility), and telling the locations of all registration papers, pedigrees, and kennel records. Just think of the possibilities which might happen otherwise! If there is another family member who shares your love of the dogs, that is good and you have less to worry about. But if your heirs are not dog-oriented, they will hardly know how to proceed or how to cope with the dogs themselves, and they may wind up disposing of or caring for your dogs in a manner that would break your heart were you around to know about it.

In our family, we have specific instructions in each of our wills for each of our dogs. A friend, also a dog person who regards her own dogs with the same concern and esteem as we do ours, has agreed to take over their care until they can be placed accordingly and will make certain that all will work out as we have planned. We have this person's name and phone number prominently displayed in our van and car and in our wallets. Our lawyer is aware of this fact. It is all spelled out in our wills. The friend has a signed check of ours to be used in case of an emergency or accident when we are traveling with the dogs; this check will be used to cover her expense to come and take over the care of our dogs should anything happen to make it impossible for us to do so. This, we feel, is the least any dog owner should do in preparation for the time our dogs suddenly find themselves without

An informal moment following the big win. "Jade" going Best in Match, Garden City, March 1982, owner-handled by Les Short of Wichita, Kansas. She was produced by Shanghai Southern Tease ex Princess Mai Lan.

Ch. Cedar Creek's Party Girl, born August 1978, by Jewell's Supermanchu ex Jemaco Meme of Cedar Creek, owned by K. Jane Weiss, Shanghai Chows, taking a 4-point major on the way to the title under Mr. Henry Stoecker at Camden County 1979.

us. There have been so many sad cases of dogs unprovided for by their loving owners, left to heirs who couldn't care less and who disposed of them in any way at all to get rid of them, or left to heirs who kept and neglected them under the misguided idea that they were providing them "a fine home with lots of freedom." All of us *must* prevent any of these misfortunes befalling our own dogs who have meant so much to us!

The start of something big! Ch. Dusten's Almond Joy at three months and already a winner. Dusten's Chow Chows, Dusten and John Cox, Sharon, Connecticut.

Index

A

Ah Sid (kennel), 48, 67, 216, 276
AHSO Fan-C (kennel), 50-76, 179, 251, 256
Al De Bear (kennel), 57-60
Allen, Hal, 80
Allen, Hal & Marie, 44
Allright, Mr., 19
Ambrose, Margaret, 211
American-bred Class, 213, 214, 215
American Kennel Club (A.K.C.), 115, 123, 127, 131, 142, 151, 212, 213, 221, 245
American Kennel Club Stud Book, 214
Amwell (kennel), 16, 19, 29
Anderson, Mrs. Agrippina, 36, 38
Anderson, John, 38
Armitage, George & Nina, 40
Atinello, Cindy, 152, 154, 171, 204
Aull, Don, 44

B

Bancroft, Mrs. Ivy, 22
Barlow, Bobby, 137
Bathing, 202, 203
Baytor (kennel), 14, 20, 21
Bechtold, Marie, 35
Bergum, Bill, 137
Bertrand, Guy, 101
Best of Breed, 221, 222, 224
Best Junior Handler, 228
Best of Opposite Sex, 221
Best in Show, 222
Best of Variety, 221
Best of Winners, 221
Biddle, Sharon, 65

Bitch, 139, 142, 150
Bite, 205, 208
Blakenship, Gary & Carmen, 186
Blue Dragon (kennel), 25
Bonnel, Mrs. Sylvia, 70
Bonney, Mrs. Leonard (Flora), 26, 31, 35, 38
The Book of the Chow Chow, 20
Boudreau, Carl, 211
Boudreau, Carl & Marcia, 70, 72, 122, 130, 140, 209, 220
Bowden, Merilyn, 37
Bowker, Mrs. Iris, 22, 23
Boxer Briefs, 7
Brace Class, 222
Brearley, Joan, 20
Bred-by-Exhibitor, 213, 213
Breech birth, 266
Breeding, 247-275
Breeding certificate, 262
Broadhurst, Florence & Douglas, 13
Brood bitch, 247-250, 252, 253
Brood Bitch Class, 223
Brushing, 198-201
Bu Dynasty (kennel), 97, 98, 110
Buckley, Mrs., 22
Burgess, Mrs., 18

C

Cabaret (kennel), 61-62, 144, 272
Caesarean section, 268
Cambellyn (kennel), 97
Campbell, James, 97, 98, 99
Campbell, Ken, 116
Canine Chronicle, 7
Caruso, Jan, 231

Casella, Miss Ella, 18
Casselberry, Jewell, 74
Castleton, Phyllis, 97, 99, 116, 140, 200, 224, 254
Cedar Creek (kennel), 64-65
Chambers, Mary Ann, 82, 136
Chambers, William, 82
Champad (kennel), 98
Chang-Shi (kennel), 41
Chapman, Beulah, 78
Charmar (kennel), 41
Cherokee (kennel), 41
Chi-Kwang (kennel), 98
The Chow Chow Club, 48-49
Chow Chow, early history in the United States, 25-49
Chow Chow, origin of, 11-13
Chow Chows in:
    Australia, 109-113
    Canada, 97-107
    Great Britain, 15-23
    United States, 25-49
Chow Life, 49
Clairedale (kennel), 31, 43
Clark, Mrs. Emma, 35
Clark, Mrs. James, 113
Cline, Susan, 148
Coat, 119, 120, 197, 208-209
Cobbiness, 123
Collar, 163
Color, 119, 120, 124
Commands, 191, 242
Companion Dog (C.D.), 244
Companion Dog Excellent (C.D.X.), 244
Coogan, Zola, 217, 128
Correll, Dawn, 94
Correll, Meribeth, 93-95, 139, 189
Cox, Dusten, 152, 171, 190, 204
Cox, Dusten & John, 2, 40, 66-69, 135, 147, 154, 160, 172, 186, 232, 276, 281
Crate, 155, 158, 211
Crisp, Mr. & Mrs. E., 41
Cunningham, Ed & Debbie, 51
Cunningham, Kimberly Ann, 207

D
Dachel, Michael, 136, 215
De Sousa, Geri, 72
Derby, Miss A.C., 25
DHL shot, 271
Dickson, Mr. & Mrs. Janvrim, 18
Disqualifications, 119, 123, 124

The Dog Fancier, 7
Dog News, 7
Dog show, enjoying the, 236-237, 240-241
Dog World, 7
Dogdom, 7
Donnelly, Rick & Reba, 132
Donnelly, Susie, 114, 126, 196, 236
Draper, Dr. Samuel, 10, 20, 24, 37, 53, 70, 75-76, 148, 230
Drennan, Donald L., 43
Durst, Barbara A., 87-91, 164, 182, 267, 268
Dusten's (kennel), 66-69, 135, 172, 186, 190, 281

E
Earle, Dr. Imogene P., 33, 240
Ely, Ronald & Kathleen, 100, 101
Emerson, Mrs. Howard, 35
Estep, Charles & Pamela, 52
Evans, Mrs. Charles, 41, 46
Ewing, Ron, 189
Exercise, 159, 265, 269
Exercise pen, 231

F
Family dog or pet dog, 134, 138, 151
Faults, 120
Feeding, 167, 193-194
    bitch, 265, 269, 271
    by hand or tube, 270
    puppies, 271
    schedule, 194
Fence, 158, 159, 162
Fitswilliam, Mrs., 18
Fitzgerald, Mrs. William L., 35
Foo H'Sing (kennel), 97
Food supplements, 193
Foods, 193
Forsyth, Jan, 34, 45, 210, 217
Foy, Marcia, 7
Frederick, Elsie, 33
Friedman, Arthur, 117, 133, 169, 174
Friedman, Barbara, 133, 169
Fritz, Dr. William, 34, 251
Fu King (kennel), 78
Futurity Stakes, 227

G
Gadston, Mr., 113
Gait, 119, 120, 123, 237, 240, 241
Garrolts, Dewain & Brenda, 52

General appearance, 118, 119
Glenmont (kennel), 36
Goodwin, Mrs. Edward H., 35
Gordon, Lady Granville, 16, 18
Gotschall (kennel), 43
Gotschall, Mrs. Valetta, 43
Graham, Florence Wilson, 41
Greenacre (kennel), 29, 35
Gregory, Joe, 44
Gregory, Mamie Reynolds, 42, 44, 214
Grooming, 197-202
Grooming equipment, 163, 198

H
Hamon, Barbara, 73, 153, 154
Hamon, Kimberly & Sharon, 73, 74
Hampton, Anne A. & Ashley, 53, 54, 261
Hampton, Anthony, 261
Hampton, Norm, 53
Hanchow (kennel), 98
Handler, 134
Hannephin, Joan, 39
Hanson, Walter, 33
Hanson, Mrs. Walter, 30, 33
Harrison, J., 23
Harter, Herold M., Jr., 35
Hartley, Mrs. Inez, 69
Hartley, Mrs. Heywood, 88
Health certificate, 249
Heckmann, Mrs. Winifred, 236
Helferich, Victoria, 51
Hellum, Ralph, 28, 32
Henson, Bonnie, 64, 65
Hetherington, Robert A., Jr., 10, 37, 75-77
Hetherington, Mrs. A., Jr., 37, 75-77, 230
Hildewell (kennel), 19
Hoisam (kennel), 112, 218
Holgate, Jack, 18
Hoover, Mrs. Earl, 32
House training, 191
Humpage, Mr. & Mrs. Frederick, 29, 40
Humphries, Mrs. Earl L., 45
Humphries, Naomi Scott, 44
Hunter, Wilma, 180
Huntley, Marquis & Marchioness, 15
Huston, Jane, 35
Hutton, Franklin, 28

I
Inbreeding, 257
Immunization shots, 271

J
James, Mrs. Arthur, 18
James, Bobby, 112, 113
Jarrett, Dr. & Mrs. Henry, 26
Joly, Mrs. Lucille, 100, 101, 187
Jones, Bert & Greta, 23
Jones, Carolyn, 46
Judging, 205, 208, 237
Junior Showmanship Class, 228
Junior Showmanship Competition, 227

K
Kamara (kennel), 70-72, 122, 130, 209, 220
Kasten, Winifred, 78
Keba-Yan (kennel), 100
Keen, Jim & Debbie, 93
Kendall, Howard, 46
Kendall, Mr. & Mrs. L. Howard, 30, 38
Kendrick, William, 46
Kennels, 134, 146
  early (U.S.), 26-49
  in U.S., 51-95
Kim-Sha (kennel), 73
Kitts, C., 65
Kobrzyck, Steve & Wendy, 117, 247
Koon, R.B., 35
Kristoff, Mrs. Barbara, 98
Krupp, Mrs. Armin, 101, 104, 105, 107, 155, 163, 175
Kuester, Mrs. Hanna K., 98, 107
Kwhy (kennel), 18
Ky-Lin, 74

L
Lakeview (kennel), 44
Lacroix, Mr. & Mrs. Maurice, 96, 101, 138, 162, 269, 276
Larizzo, Mike, 76, 238
Leash, 163
Leavitt, Michael, 71, 241
Ledgelands (kennel), 28
Lenfesty, Nancy, 37
Leunissen-Rooseboom, H.L. & J., 127, 128, 132
Liontamer, 75-77, 79
Lincoln, Mrs. E.K., 29, 41
Line-breeding, 257
Litter, 266, 267, 268
Lonsdale, Earl of (Lord Hugh), 15
Loy-Jean (kennel), 37

M

MacEachern, Mary, 44
MacMonnies, Mr., 41
Maibach, Mr. & Mrs. Cecil, 28
Mandarin (kennel), 27
Manooch, Mrs., 32
Marcy, Renee, 140, 254
Marra, Mrs. Waldo, Jr., 35
Marston, Joel, 38, 44, 56, 60
Match shows, 213
Mating, 247, 243, 260-261, 264
McEachern, Mrs., N.V., 100
Meaney, Audrey & Richard, 12, 216
Meisner, Nancy, 100
Messer, Floyd & Jean, 39
Messmore, Mrs. A.F., 35
Messnarz, D. & C., 112, 113, 218
Meyer, Mrs. Marie B., 214
Millet, Jeanne, 43
Millit, Mrs., 23
Minsh (kennel), 101, 107, 155, 159
Mi-Pao (kennel), 98, 107
Moore, Andrea, Mrs., 49
Morgan, Marilyn Bowden, 75
Munson, Bryon, 91
Murphy, Desmond J., 9, 75, 76, 114,
   124, 126, 133, 148, 168, 174, 189, 196,
   197, 236, 238
Murray, Ken, 162

N

Nattrass, Mrs. M.J., 98
Newcombe, Margaret P., 31, 43
Nicholas, Anna Katherine, 7-9, 176, 189
Nicholas Guide to Dog Judging, 8
North, Dr. & Mrs. Edward, 44
Novice Class, 213, 214
Nylabone®, 166

O

Obedience, 243-245
Obedience titles, 244-245
Obedience Trial Champion (O.T. Ch.), 245
Oberstar, Frank, 189
Odenkirchen, F.P.A., 96, 98, 101
Onken, Mrs., 18
Open Class, 215
Open Junior Showmanship Class, 227
Outcrossing, 258

P

Pagemoor (kennel), 29

Palm, Earl, 78-79
Palm, Mae, 76, 78-79, 124, 162, 168, 238
Palm (kennel), 78-79
Parrish, Sarah, 80-81, 225, 235, 238, 274
Patten, Misses, 27
Peck, Miss Anna, 19
Peddie, Mr. J.C.F., 97, 176
Pedigree, 146, 151, 248, 253, 256, 271
Penney, Claire Knapp (Mrs. Claire
   Dixon), 31, 43
Pennydale (kennel), 31
Pennyworth (kennel), 48
Perkinson, Laura, 92, 164
Perry, Vincent, 91
Peters, Harry T., 28
Phillips, Lady Faudel, 15, 16, 18, 19, 29
Pierce, Ruby, 242
Point shows, 213
Poppyland (kennel), 38
Popular Dogs, 7
Porter, K.L., 79, 162
Pregnancy, 265
Pre-show preparation, 228, 231-233
Preston, Mrs. Marvin, 35
Prinz, Mrs. Anny, 35
Proctor, Mrs. Charles E., 25
Propp, Keith, 93
Pugh, Mrs. Hilda, 97
Puppy, 155, 158-159, 162-163, 166-167,
   170, 174-175, 178, 182-183, 186-187,
   190-191, 193-194
Puppy and children, 166-167
Puppy Class, 213
Purchase, 131, 134, 139, 142-143, 146,
   150-151
Pure-Bred Dogs/American Kennel Gazette,
   7, 221

R

Reed, Mrs. C.J., 108, 109, 110, 111, 142,
   260, 262
Registration, 213
Regulations for Junior Showmanship, 228
Reife, John, 180
Reimers, Thea, 267
Rensink, Ken, 189
Reserve, 217
Responsibilities (owners, breeders), 277,
   278, 280
Reynolds, Davis S., 44
Richard, James, 61-62, 144, 244
Richard, Jamie, 61, 63, 144

Richard, Joan, 61-62, 244, 272
Robb, R.D., 98
Robb, Mr. & Mrs., 176
Roberts, John, 56
Robson, Mrs. Alan, 137, 169, 176
Rodriques, Fernando, 16
Rosenberg, Alva, 43
Rowles, John, 113

S

Sa-Mi (kennel), 80-81, 274
Sanders, Lorraine, 138
Scaramanga, Mrs., 18, 25
Schneider, M., 162
Schwartz, Alexander, 168
Schwartz, Mrs. Alexander C., Jr., 77
Scriven, William, 20
Seamer, Mrs. Louise, 32
Sedna (kennel), 108-112, 142, 260, 262
Seligman, Dr. Leon, 195
"Set up" or "stack," 237
Seward, Betty Mae, 67, 74
Shanghai (kennel), 84-86, 135, 143, 179, 183, 199, 252
Short, Les, 257, 279
Short, Les & Marilyn, 50, 51-52, 54-56, 233, 251, 256
Short, Marilyn, 179, 180
Sho-Tay (kennel), 82-83
Show dog, 142-143, 150-151, 205-241
Show Dogs, 7
Shyrock, Clif & Vivian, 44
Simpson, Liz, 110
Sinkiang (kennel), 100
Size, 120, 123
Smith, Elizabeth, 238
Smooth-coated Chow Chow, 127-128
Socializing, 174-175, 178, 182-183, 205
Spaying, 139, 142
Specials, 221, 222
Speers, Frances, 64-65, 242, 263
Spies, Hermann P., 101, 138
Spike, Ralph W., 33
Spike, Mrs. Ralph, 33, 38
Stamm, Alan & Delores, 57-60, 230, 235
Standards, 115
    American, 118-119
    Australian, 119-120
    British, 119-120
Standards, interpretation of American, 120-121, 123, 124
Staple, Miss Kathleen, 31, 35

Starcrest (kennel), 44, 60
Sterling, Jerry & Lucille, 40
Stine, Kenneth, 45
Stoecker, Henry, 164, 280
Stolzenbach, Kathleen & Kurt, 154, 171
Stonybrook (kennel), 75, 124, 168, 238
Stud dog, 253, 256, 264
Stud Dog Class, 222
Stud fee, 248, 253
Successful Dog Show Exhibiting, 227
Sunnybrook (kennel), 76
Sunswept (kennel), 87, 91, 182, 268
Suyan (kennel), 98
Sweepstakes, 227

T

Taichung (kennel), 192, 164
Talkington, Kate, 182
Tally Ho (kennel), 26
Tartar dog (man kou), 11
Taunton, W.K., 17
Taylor, William, 189
Teeth, 118, 211
Temple, W., 18
Thompson, A., 143
Thompson, Nancy, 206
Toys, 166, 167
Tracking Dog (T.D.), 245
Tracking Dog Excellent (T.D.X.), 245
Training, 186-187, 190-191
Trainor, William, 217, 218
Transport (bitch), 248-250, 252
Travel, 208, 249, 273-275

U

Ullman, Jill, 82
Utility Dog (U.D.), 244

V

Valcourt, Gaston, 27
Van Dusen Volkstadt, Bessie, 43
Vandeventer, Mrs., 53
Variety Group, 222
Vaudo, Joseph, A., Jr., 226
Vaudo, Mary, 217, 218
Veldhuis, Mrs. Christina A., 127
Veterans Class, 224

W

Wagstaff, Mr. & Mrs. David, 28, 32, 35
Wakeman, Mrs. Sheila, 113
Waller, Mr. & Mrs., E.C., 28

Walton, Mrs., 64
Warnsborn (kennel), 127
Weight, 120, 123
Weiss, K. Jane, 50, 54, 84-86, 135, 143,
    157, 164, 179, 183, 195, 199, 252, 281
Wellborn, Joan, 36, 40, 43, 67, 276
West, O.H., 33
Westlake, Anita H., 14, 16, 17, 19, 20,
    21, 22
Westlake, Jennifer, 19, 22
Whelping, 265, 266
Whelping box, 265
Whitaker, Percy, 16
Wiesman, Mrs. Madge P., 97
Williams, Herb, 93, 95, 97, 110
Williams, Joan, 93, 95, 97, 176
Wills, Robert, 52, 225

Winners Class, 217
Winners Bitch, 217, 221
Winners Dog, 217, 221
Wold, Michael, 137, 174
Wolf, Michael, 92, 117, 133, 169, 174,
    254
Worms, 271
Wu-Li (kennel), 92, 93-94

Y
Yan Paul, Mrs., 98
Yan Fu (kennel), 32
Young, Ted, Jr., 77, 230

Z
Ziegler, O.B., 35